W9-BLP-589

FLASH!

THE ASSOCIATED PRESS
COVERS THE WORLD

WITHDRAWN

FLASH!

THE ASSOCIATED PRESS COVERS THE WORLD

INTRODUCTION BY PETER ARNETT

EDITED BY VINCENT ALABISO,
KELLY SMITH TUNNEY AND CHUCK ZOELLER

THE ASSOCIATED PRESS IN ASSOCIATION WITH
HARRY N. ABRAMS, INC., PUBLISHERS

For Harry N. Abrams, Inc.:
PROJECT MANAGER: ERIC HIMMEL
EDITOR: RACHEL TSUTSUMI
DESIGNER: RAYMOND P. HOOPER

Library of Congress Cataloging-in-Publication Data

Flash! : the Associated Press covers the world / by the Associated
    Press ; introduction by Peter Arnett.
        p.   cm.
    Includes index.
    ISBN 0–8109–1974–5 (clothbound) / ISBN 0–8109–2793–4 (pbk.)
    1. Associated Press.   2. Journalism—United States.   3. Press—
United States.   I. Associated Press.
PN4841.A85F56   1998
070.4'35—DC21   97–40307

Copyright © The Associated Press, 1998
Published in 1998 by Harry N. Abrams, Incorporated, New York
All rights reserved. No part of the contents of this book may be reproduced
without the written permission of the publisher

Printed and bound in Italy

 Harry N. Abrams, Inc.
100 Fifth Avenue
New York, N.Y. 10011
www.abramsbooks.com

Front cover: see pages 124–25
Back cover: see pages 8–9
Frontispiece: negative of photograph on pages 8–9

CONTENTS

NEW YORK, MAY 10, 1940 – Pedestrians strain to view the latest news on an AP teletype machine in a window outside AP headquarters at 50 Rockefeller Plaza.

DEDICATION

This book celebrates the story of The Associated Press, whose men and women have witnessed and recorded history for 150 years.

Readers will recognize many of the photographs as icons of the past—distant as well as recent. Some will bring a smile of recollection, others a tear of sadness.

The text tells the story of a vast global news enterprise that still operates by the rules that gave it life in 1848: Get it first, get it fast, get it right. And be fair.

Only a few of the heroes of this tale are mentioned in these pages, a few exploits cited to tell the story of the AP—the greatest single source of news in the world. In the end, it is the story of news.

In our 150 years, 23 AP people have died in the line of duty. We have won 43 Pulitzer Prizes. In tragedy and triumph, generations of AP people have dedicated their lives to this enterprise, as proud to be a part of it as we are of them.

So we dedicate this book to tens of thousands of AP men and women, of the past and of the present, who have made it possible for the AP to become the backbone of the nation's news and a voice that reaches around the world.

That includes all the staff—the technical experts who keep us at the frontier, the unsung administrators and marketers who work far from the headlines but without whom we could not build and manage a worldwide news company, and so many others whose talents keep the AP humming all day every day everywhere.

And it is dedicated as well to the newspaper and broadcast "members" of this not-for-profit news cooperative, whose ancestors gave birth to the AP at the tip of Manhattan Island a century and a half ago and without whom the AP would not be what it is today—the largest news organization in the world.

News is our story. We hope you enjoy reading and seeing it.

Louis D. Boccardi
President and Chief Executive Officer

Iwo Jima, Volcano Islands, Feb. 23, 1945 —
U.S. Marines raise the flag atop Mount Suribachi
on the Pacific island of Iwo Jima in World War II.
Joe Rosenthal
Pulitzer Prize

LAKEHURST, N.J., MAY 6, 1937 – The German zeppelin *Hindenburg* crashes to the ground after bursting into flames while preparing to dock. Thirty-five passengers and crew died, including one crew member on the ground.

St. Louis, Nov. 4, 1948 – President Harry S. Truman holds up an Election Day edition of the *Chicago Daily Tribune,* which, based on early results, mistakenly announced "Dewey Defeats Truman." The president told well-wishers in St. Louis, "That is one for the books!"

Byron Rollins

NEW YORK, JULY 4, 1939 – New York Yankees'
Lou Gehrig, the "Iron Horse," wipes away a tear
during a sold-out tribute at Yankee Stadium.
Gehrig's record-breaking career was cut short by
a rare neuromuscular disease.

Murray Becker

SAIGON, VIETNAM, FEB. 1, 1968 – South Vietnamese National Police Chief Nguyen Ngoc Loan summarily executes a suspected member of the Viet Cong captured in Saigon during the communist Tet Offensive.

Eddie Adams
Pulitzer Prize

EYEWITNESS TO HISTORY
By Peter Arnett

I lay flat on my back in a Saigon alley with a trio of plainclothes police tattooing my face with their fists. They were enraged at reporters covering an unlicensed anti-government Buddhist rally—and they pounced on me because I was the smallest target. Through a red mist I saw my Associated Press colleague, Malcolm Browne, himself under assault by the police, snap pictures of my misery. David Halberstam of *The New York Times* eventually shouldered his way through the tormentors and dragged me to safety.

"Great pictures," Browne said as he dusted off my bloody shirt while we hurried back to the AP bureau to file the story. "Sorry you had to suffer through it." Mal Browne didn't allow his personal feelings to intrude, even though a colleague's head was being bashed in. It was news, after all, that the Saigon police in these early days of the Vietnam War were being unleashed against the American press.

I knew there was a basic doctrine of the AP that the reporter should stay out of the story. Lesson one is if you're an eyewitness to history, be clearheaded and impartial. But on that bloody morning in Saigon I knew we had caught the police being bullies, acting toward us as they had their own people. It was a story worth getting involved in.

In looking back on my 20 years with the AP, I realized that it was frequently impossible to avoid becoming involved in the story. The assault in a Saigon back alley was the inevitable consequence of the AP asserting its right to cover anything, anywhere. I got a lacerated skull out of it, but Mal Browne's account of the event—and the other confrontations that followed—helped propel American policy toward a traumatic showdown with the Saigon government. Not only were we eyewitnesses to history, by our presence we influenced it.

That was heady stuff for me, a 28-year-old reporter, squaring off against the repressive authorities in Vietnam. It set a journalistic course for a lifetime. The longer I worked for the AP, the more it became clear to me that my experience was not that unusual, that as a rain shower ultimately affects the level of the oceans, so does the presence of a reporter influence the flow of history. The more I learned about the AP, the more I realized that it was always this way.

The first AP Washington correspondent, Lawrence Gobright, wrote in the days when newspapers and the nation were choosing up sides for the Civil War. He explained, "My business is to communicate facts; my instructions do not allow me to make any comment upon the facts that I communicate . . . my dispatches are merely dry matters of fact and detail." But Gobright's professional detachment did not sit well in the fevered world of politics of that time, and he commented, "Although I try to write without regard to men or politics, I do not always escape censure."

Writing "without regard to men or politics" is a phrase easy to say but exacting to implement. It's what the AP does.

I learned this truth about the AP soon after I joined the news cooperative in the 1960s as a reporter. I was a tiny cog in a vast news machine that was then producing around 3 million words a day and hundreds of pictures. The stream of information poured through a network of

MEKONG DELTA, VIETNAM, SEPTEMBER 1965 – AP Saigon photographer Huynh Thanh My is pinned down in a rice paddy with the Vietnamese unit he is covering during the war. The 29-year-old was killed a month later, when the Vietnamese battalion he was with was attacked by the Viet Cong.

teletype, cable and radio circuits that linked newspapers, radio and television stations in more than 100 countries. To a greenhorn newsman like me, that was an intimidating responsibility.

I felt far distant from AP's New York headquarters half a world away, linked to my base in Jakarta, Indonesia, by an antiquated Morse code system tap-tapping across the ocean of verbiage. I worried endlessly over the meager few hundred words I sent every day or so about President Sukarno, a melodramatic neutralist leader then courted by both sides in the Cold War. Acquaintances warned me that the local authorities were sensitive.

Despite my care, I soon fell afoul of the government for writing realistic accounts of the rapidly deteriorating economy. I was expelled. I departed Jakarta convinced my wire service career was over. But the AP's regional chief, Don Huth, was at the Singapore airport to meet me and offered a supportive hug. "Hey, we're on your side," he said. He handed me a message from AP President Frank Starzel saying I'd done a great job. I was asked if I wanted to go to Vietnam. Need I say I was enamored with the AP forever?

Of course, it's a two-way street this trust thing. You make a pact with the AP and you are hooking into news traditions that can make the most extreme demands on you. That's what I discovered in Vietnam.

Vietnam was where I watched men dying for The Associated Press, and worked alongside others willing to risk it. It's one thing to put on your nation's uniform to give your life for your country. But to dress up in black-market khakis and head into battle in a borrowed bush hat, armed only with a Nikon camera, 10 rolls of film and a notebook, is definitely another thing. I covered the Vietnam War for years with an unshakable belief in my own immortality. But what about the diminutive Huynh Thanh My, who signed up for numerous photographic forays into the swamps and jungles to eventually die a terrible death, leaving behind a young widow and a baby daughter?

And Ollie Noonan, a happy-go-lucky freelancer, whose dearest wish was to take pictures for the AP, a dying wish it turned out. Likewise Bernard Kolenberg. Or Henri Huet, the most gentle of colleagues, whose cameras captured some of the most sensitive images of the war, cameras that were consumed with him in the fiery crash of a helicopter.

What kind of organization can ask that of a person, to permit the risking of life itself for something as transitory as a news story? At a time when the death of even one American soldier can lead to national anguish, where does the AP find the courage to ask people to risk their lives in the pursuit of news? Six AP men and women have died these past four years.

On reflection, I would say that only a news organization that is very, very sure of its mission can ask its employees to routinely do this. To me, that separates the AP from the rest of the news industry.

AP reporters are expected to be wherever the news is happening, from routine legislative sessions in Baton Rouge to bloody massacres in Burundi. That is the covenant the organization has with the more than 1,500 newspapers and 6,000 television and radio outlets it serves in the United States, all of which are members under the AP's unique cooperative structure and all of which rely on its 24-hour news reports. The responsibility weighs heavily on AP reporters and executives because when undertaken forthrightly it can require coverage decisions involving great danger. The organization has always managed to find staffers willing to serve its needs, whatever the risk.

Because of this tradition of commitment, the AP news report has become the blood that flows through the body of American journalism, an essential component in the nation's news day.

The AP was not always so indomitable. It was born a child of convenience by six New York newspapers intent on reducing news-gathering costs in a joint venture. The first modest plans for the AP included supplying routine shipping and market reports. The organization grew with the American news industry, but remained a not-for-profit news cooperative. It eventually supplied general and comprehensive news services that no paper alone could afford to maintain. Today at 150 years the AP is the oldest and largest news-gathering organization of its kind in the world, serving more than 15,000 newspaper and broadcast outlets worldwide.

The 20 million words the AP now spills across its wires every day are an endeavor, according to an old company history, "to report on human effort and events with insight and detachment, giving readers a firm basis of facts by which to form their own judgment."

I always liked the phrase "a firm basis of facts by which to form their own judgment." It's one of the stanchions of American democracy. That's what the Founding Fathers intended when they wrote into the Constitution the unique concept of freedom of the press. That's why I think that it is in the terms of American democracy that the AP should be judged in its 150th year.

If democracy is the voice of the people, then the AP is its stenographer. From its humdrum "basic mission" of covering routine spot news events of the day, through the deliberations of elected officials and on to natural and man-made disasters, the AP takes the pulse of American life, and increasingly the world's. It has become a marvel of the information age with its high-tech gadgetry that moves news and pictures everywhere, instantly. The AP product fills as much as 65 percent of some of America's daily newspapers.

There are high-tech news competitors trying to invade the AP's domain as free-market forces cruise the information superhighway. And as King of the Hill, the AP has its critics. The cooperative is expected to be on top of every major news story, and competitive in enterprise and investigative reporting as well. Some wish it to be as erudite as *The New York Times*, others as flashy as CNN. The AP toils to live up to these expectations and generally succeeds but sometimes fails. Yet in its dedication and consistency, the AP is incomparable, a strong partner to American democracy.

By reporting America's history across 150 years, the AP has become entwined in its threads. The news cooperative zealously charted the troubled course of nationhood, and in those early days was often alone. The Civil War was typical. It was an AP staffer who reported Lincoln's farewell to Springfield, an AP agent who covered the shelling and surrender of Fort Sumter. The AP took down by hand and ran in full the Gettysburg Address, although few papers printed it. It was an AP man who, minutes after Lincoln's assassination, held Booth's weapon in his hand, reconstructed the events and reported the awful facts that set the nation on fire.

Privileged eyewitnesses to the nation's and the world's history. . . . In wars where two nations fought, the AP covered the battle from both sides. When the Japanese fought the Russians at the turn of the 20th century, and an AP reporter took a bullet while covering the Russian side, his AP replacement was drawn from the Japanese lines and had to trek hundreds of miles around the battle scene to his new assignment.

Whenever the United States took up arms, there were AP reporters at the front. In the Spanish-American War, when victorious American troops entered Santiago, Cuba, there was an AP man there to greet them. In World War I, it was an AP reporter who was handed the secret German proposal to ally Germany with Mexico to outflank the United States. An AP photographer captured the sudden hell that was the zeppelin *Hindenburg*, the pride of Nazi Germany, a burning hulk at Lakehurst, N.J.

In the 1930s, while Hitler and Mussolini wrestled smaller nations to the ground, AP reporters covered these machinations from Albania to Czechoslovakia, from Ethiopia to Spain. They splashed ashore on D-Day, and throughout World War II these photographers and writers caught the symbols of war, the body-strewn sands of Tarawa, the marching ranks of GIs filling the Champs Elysees as if emerging from the Arc de Triomphe. And it was the AP's Joe Rosenthal whose camera caught the Marines raising the Stars and Stripes on Mount Suribachi, the most reprinted picture in history, made into a 3-cent postage stamp when 3 cents would deliver the mail, and later a memorial in the nation's capital.

In Korea, a captured AP photographer, imprisoned by the North Koreans, smuggled out clandestinely snapped pictures of his fellow prisoners of war. When Little Rock High School was integrated, an AP man dictated a Pulitzer Prize-winning story from a phone booth paces away. It was an AP photographer who froze in the American mind the image of wounded civil rights activist James Meredith, grimacing in pain on a Mississippi road, shotgunned during his attempt to show fellow blacks there was nothing to fear in protest.

In my years with the AP I thrilled to its legends and dreamed of emulating its heroes. My favorite reporter was Mark Kellogg, a string correspondent for the cooperative, just as I had been in my earlier years. He drew the assignment to cover Colonel George Custer's regiment as it rode in the Badlands to punish Sitting Bull and his warlike Sioux. Kellogg's handwritten accounts were dispatched across the plains by pony to a telegraph office many miles away.

On June 24, 1876, Kellogg wrote in his last dispatch, "By the time this reaches you we would have met and fought the red devils, with what result remains to be seen. I go with Custer and will be at the death." And he was. There are those who might argue that Kellogg was a fool to ride with Custer in the first place, and would have been better advised to have covered the Indian Wars from regimental headquarters. How far to go is always a question in times of crisis, and we all gamble with our lives a little. Ninety-nine years after the Battle of the Little Bighorn I was covering a military debacle that had similar overtones of disas-

ter for the United States. I was in chaotic Saigon, a city about to fall to victorious communist North Vietnamese troops as the last Americans fled. With me were AP's George Esper and Matt Franjola, waiting to cover the end. We felt close to history and to Mark Kellogg. But our gamble succeeded and we got out alive and with the story.

Twenty-three AP reporters didn't get out alive in the course of the last 150 years, and you could argue that every one of them could have been in some safer place. That they were willingly in the line of fire says much for their confidence in the mission of the news cooperative they worked for, and their belief in the value of their journalism. That the spirit of sacrifice lives on was revealed to me in the days after the young AP photographer Hansi Krauss was killed by a Somali mob while covering the civil war near Mogadishu in 1993. London photo editor Horst Faas later told me that a dozen photographers volunteered to replace Krauss immediately on that most dangerous of assignments.

There are others in the AP whose life-threatening experiences also remind us that news gathering can come at a high personal price. These reporters were thrust into perilous circumstances with little warning, and had to draw on deep resources of courage and integrity to survive. The most stirring example is that of Middle East correspondent Terry Anderson, kidnapped in Beirut in 1985 and held hostage by terrorists for six and a half long years before his release. His ordeal created a bond among journalists throughout the world. There are risks in covering much of the world.

Reid Miller was a veteran bureau chief in

the AP domestic service in the early 1980s when he volunteered for duty in Central America covering the dirty little wars then disrupting the region. In May of 1984, Miller and other reporters were called to a routine news conference by Eden Pastora, a rebel leader fighting the Sandinistas. But the conference near the remote San Juan River was disrupted by an explosion that tore through the assembled journalists. Miller and many of the other wounded crawled or stumbled from the building and were sitting or lying on the muddy riverbank awaiting assistance.

One of those was Linda Frazier, the wife of the AP's Central American correspondent Joe Frazier. She was working for the *Tico Times* of San Jose, Costa Rica, and mother to a 10-year-old son. Miller observed, "Linda was pulled from the house almost an hour after the explosion and laid on a blanket nearby. Mortally wounded, she was to lie there another two hours before help came, a doctor and two nurses dressed in the green fatigues of Pastora's Revolutionary Democratic Alliance. She and all the other wounded received an injection of an antibiotic, but little else.

"At one point, I crawled over to her, unable to walk because of the shrapnel wounds in my right leg. She took my hand and I could see she was talking to me but I could not hear her words because the explosion had left me temporarily deaf. I learned later that she had died."

Miller recovered from his wounds and remained in Central America for most of the decade before volunteering for a post in Africa, a continent where many leaders were notorious for their animosity toward the press.

It was in the Central African Republic in July 1977 that correspondent Michael Goldsmith was arrested by secret police under the mistaken impression he was a South African spy. He was driven from the capital, Bangui, 70 miles to Berengo, the birthplace and residence of Jean-Bedel Bokassa, the self-proclaimed emperor. Bokassa carried a heavy embossed stick that served as his scepter.

Goldsmith had been trying in vain to interview Bokassa. Now he was certain that a simple explanation would clear up this ugly mess. Bokassa looked at him wordlessly. Goldsmith bowed and said, "Your Majesty." Bokassa raised his stick and brought it down full force on Goldsmith's forehead, opening a large gash. The 55-year-old AP reporter fell to the ground unconscious. He came to seconds later, now being kicked brutally by Bokassa and his guards. "I saw my spectacles lying on the ground, inches from my face. I heard a raucous voice say, 'There are his spectacles. Crush them.' A boot came down heavily on them and I saw the glasses splinter into fragments." He discovered later it was the emperor's boot.

Goldsmith was still bleeding from his wounds when he woke sometime the next day in his cell. He had been stripped to his shorts and had only a crude cement slab for a bed. For six days he lived with his festering and untreated wounds. Once a day the steel door was opened and he was given water and a piece of manioc, the starchy, tasteless root that is part of the African diet. Outside his door was a perpetual guard of six soldiers armed with submachine guns. It was days before he realized he was back in the capital. He pleaded in French in vain for medical aid and contact with the U.S. Embassy. He was answered with jeers and further brutalities.

Goldsmith's treatment eventually improved, and one month to the day after his arrest he was freed. But Bokassa was not done with him yet. The reporter was taken to the royal palace, where Bokassa said it was the eloquent pleas of Goldsmith's wife, Roxanne, that persuaded him to release Goldsmith. Surrounded by some 20 of his children and a dozen ministers, the emperor spoke without interruption for three hours, repeatedly saying it was the love of Goldsmith's wife that had saved his life and that henceforth he would regard them both as members of his entourage. With that, Bokassa kissed Goldsmith three times on each cheek and let him depart.

My own journalistic crisis came not from deliberate physical abuse or accidental injury but from a smear campaign against my coverage of the Vietnam War that began as a whisper in Saigon and became a roar bellowed out by Lyndon Baines Johnson in the Oval Office of the White House. That the president of the United States was so angered by the war coverage that he ordered the FBI to investigate me and sev-

NUREMBERG, GERMANY, OCT. 1, 1946 – AP correspondent Wes Gallagher (right) bolts from the courtroom for a telephone to dictate news of the conviction and death sentences of 12 Nazi war criminals. Gallagher's wife, Betty, held an open telephone line 100 feet away from the courtroom, allowing Gallagher a one-minute beat over competitive news services. Gallagher went on to serve as the AP's president and general manager. He retired in 1976.

B.I. Sanders

eral other journalists is a matter of historical record, but what is less known is the role the AP played in clearing my name.

The Vietnam War was a defining moment for American journalism because a new generation of war correspondents severed the accommodating relationship their predecessors had forged with the military in two world wars, and instead demanded accountability. It was a struggle for press freedom fought not only by the score or more of AP staffers on the battlefield, but also at AP headquarters, a 14-story Indiana limestone building in New York's Rockefeller Plaza, known in the news cooperative as "50 Rock."

Presiding over the AP at that time was one of the most dynamic executives in the organization's history, Wes Gallagher, who had moved up the ranks from editing and writing and had been a distinguished correspondent in World War II. He visited Vietnam often, supported the staff with financial and equipment resources and, more importantly, backed our controversial coverage that deviated from the positive Washington line that the war was going well.

In one of his many pronouncements of support, Gallagher wrote, "There is an Orwellian '1984' concept, both among government officials and some segments of the public, that if the reporter just reported the good news, somehow things would be better. This is sometimes equated with patriotism by more extreme advocates. But this is not how a democracy functions. Nor could it and still remain a democracy."

My favorite Gallagher story is about his lunch with Lyndon Johnson in the White House late in 1966, the day after the president had complained to two visiting AP managing editors about my coverage in Vietnam.

They were a formidable pair, both tall and tough-minded. With the luncheon nearing an end with no mention of the war, Gallagher said:

"Mr. President, I understand you have been critical of some of AP's stories from Vietnam."

"Oh no," the president replied. "I think the AP is doing a great job."

Not willing to challenge the president on what had been reported the day before by the managing editors, Gallagher said:

"Well, I just want you to know, Mr. President, that the AP is not against you or for you."

"That is not quite the way I like it," the president replied.

One of the toughest decisions I ever made was to publicly criticize the AP for killing one of my news stories about American soldiers looting a village. It was written during the U.S. invasion of Cambodia in 1970. Wes Gallagher took responsibility for the decision—and much of the critical flak. He reconsidered, and restored the story. I knew I was acting on a matter of important prin-

ciple, but let's face it, it was like spitting on a beloved member of the family.

I quit the AP in 1981 to try my hand at television news, and went from being an AP staffer to a member. I have "ripped and read" many an AP story on the air when we've been too busy to get all the facts ourselves, and we rarely give the news cooperative any credit. That's one of the reasons the AP remains relatively unknown to the public. The industry it serves doesn't give it enough public credit.

But current AP President Louis D. Boccardi says his primary goal is to keep the trust of the news industry. When news breaks, Boccardi says, for generations newsrooms and news desks have asked, " 'Well, what does the AP say?' It's a signal of our importance in the news flow and their trust in us."

In his 12 years at the helm, Boccardi has increasingly asserted the AP's leadership role in world news coverage, and has spoken out strongly against press restrictions of any kind. Just as Lawrence Gobright covered Washington in the 1860s fairly and "without regard to men or politics," so does Boccardi insist, with Somalia and Bosnia in mind, that the press be free to cover all world crises without regard to the consequences of the coverage. It's tough enough being reporters without the role of diplomat or statesman thrown in, he says. "That envisages a role we cannot possibly play. We should reject it. Let the governors govern, let the reporters report."

Let the reporters report. Sounds to me like a clarion call for the next 150 years of The Associated Press.

LEADERSHIP

WASHINGTON, APRIL 17, 1956 – President Dwight D. Eisenhower laughs as his wife, Mamie, tries on a cardboard eyeshade during a Republican campaign dinner. Eisenhower was preparing to run for his second term in the White House.

Bob Schutz

LOS ANGELES, JULY 9, 1960 – U.S. presidential candidate John F. Kennedy is surrounded by supporters and the press as he arrives for the Democratic National Convention.

Uncredited

DALLAS, Nov. 22, 1963 – The presidential limousine carrying mortally wounded President John F. Kennedy races toward the hospital moments after he was shot. Mrs. John Connally, wife of the governer of Texas, bends over her wounded husband, and Mrs. Kennedy, center, slumps over her husband. Secret Service agent Clinton Hill rides on the back of the car.

Justin Newman

DALLAS, NOV. 22, 1963 – Lee Harvey Oswald sits in police custody shortly after being arrested for assassinating President John F. Kennedy in Dallas. Oswald was shot and killed two days later by Jack Ruby, a local club owner, as he was being transferred to a city jail.

Uncredited

ARLINGTON, VA., NOV. 25, 1963 – During funeral services at Arlington National Cemetery, Jacqueline Kennedy, widow of assassinated President John F. Kennedy, accepts the flag that covered her husband's coffin.

Eddie Adams

MONTGOMERY, ALA., MARCH 22, 1956 – The Rev.
Martin Luther King Jr. is welcomed with a kiss
from his wife, Coretta, after leaving court. King
was found guilty of conspiracy to boycott city
buses in a campaign to desegregate the bus system. A judge suspended his $500 fine pending
appeal.

Gene Herrick

HERNANDO, MISS., JUNE 6, 1966 – Civil rights activist James Meredith grimaces in pain as he pulls himself across Highway 51 after being shot during a voting rights march from Memphis, Tenn., to Jackson, Miss. Meredith, who defied segregation to enroll at the University of Mississippi in 1962, completed the march after treatment of his wounds.

Jack Thornell
Pulitzer Prize

MONTGOMERY, ALA., FEB. 22, 1956 – Rosa Parks, whose refusal to move to the back of a bus touched off the Montgomery bus boycotts and the beginning of the civil rights movement, is fingerprinted by Deputy Sheriff D.H. Lackey. She was among some 100 people who were charged with violating segregation laws.

Gene Herrick

31

BOMBAY, INDIA, JULY 6, 1946 – A bespectacled Mohandas Gandhi, the Mahatma, who eventually led India to its independence, enjoys a laugh with the man who was to be the nation's first prime minister, Jawaharlal Nehru. The occasion was a committee meeting at the All-India Congress.

Max Desfor

NEW DELHI, INDIA, JAN. 31, 1948 – The body of assassinated Indian leader Mohandas Gandhi, covered with rose petals, is carried to the site of his cremation.

Max Desfor

MUNICH, GERMANY, DEC. 5, 1931 – Adolf Hitler, leader of the National Socialists, emerges from the party's Munich headquarters. Hitler predicted his Nazi party would one day control Germany.

Uncredited

NUREMBERG, GERMANY, APRIL 23, 1945 – Tanks of the U.S. 7th Army rumble through Nuremberg, which was reduced to rubble by bombing raids and artillery fire during World War II.

Jim Pringle

WASHINGTON, APRIL 22, 1954 – U.S. Sen. Joseph McCarthy holds both hands over microphones as he speaks to his chief counsel, Roy Cohn, during a hearing of the Senate Investigations Subcommittee. The subcommittee was investigating McCarthy's dispute with top Army officials.

Byron Rollins

MATANZAS, CUBA, JAN. 6, 1959 – American television host Ed Sullivan meets with Cuban leader Fidel Castro.

Harold Valentine

THURMONT, MD., APRIL 22, 1961 – President John F. Kennedy, left, discusses the failed U.S.-backed invasion at Cuba's Bay of Pigs with his predecessor, former President Dwight D. Eisenhower, as the two walked at the Camp David presidential retreat.

Paul Vathis
Pulitzer Prize

WASHINGTON, AUG. 9, 1974 – On the day of his resignation Richard M. Nixon waves goodbye from the steps of his helicopter as he leaves the White House following a farewell address to his staff.

Chick Harrity

Moscow, Dec. 11, 1988 – Members of the Politburo vote to oust Andrei Gromyko, front center, as Soviet president, clearing the way for Communist Party chief Mikhail Gorbachev, front right, to become the new head of state.

Boris Yurchenko

ROSTOV, RUSSIA, JUNE 10, 1996 – Russian President Boris Yeltsin dances at a rock concert during his successful campaign for re-election.

Alexander Zemlianichenko
Pulitzer Prize

CHICAGO, AUG. 28, 1968 – Chicago Mayor Richard Daley shows his displeasure as shouts of Vietnam War protesters resound inside the International Amphitheater, site of the Democratic National Convention. Some politicians urged unsuccessfully that the convention be adjourned due to street demonstrations.

Uncredited

WASHINGTON, FEB. 26, 1973 – Israeli Prime Minister Golda Meir makes a point at a news conference as she arrived for talks with President Richard M. Nixon.

Bob Daugherty

PAARL, SOUTH AFRICA, FEB. 11, 1990 – Nelson Mandela and his wife, Winnie, celebrate the anti-apartheid leader's release from Victor Verster Prison after more than 27 years in jail.

Greg English

SOWETO, SOUTH AFRICA, APRIL 27, 1994 – Long lines of voters queue outside a polling station in the black township of Soweto waiting to cast ballots in South Africa's first all-race elections. Nelson Mandela was elected president.

Denis Farrell

WASHINGTON, MARCH 31, 1981 – President Ronald Reagan is shot and wounded in an assassination attempt by John Hinckley Jr. while leaving the Washington Hilton hotel. In a series of photographs, AP White House photographer Ron Edmonds captures Reagan waving, reacting to the shots and being shoved into his limousine by Secret Service agents. In the picture on the opposite page, Secret Service agent Timothy J. McCarthy, foreground, police officer Thomas K. Delahanty, center, and presidential press secretary James Brady, background, lie wounded.

Ron Edmonds
Pulitzer Prize

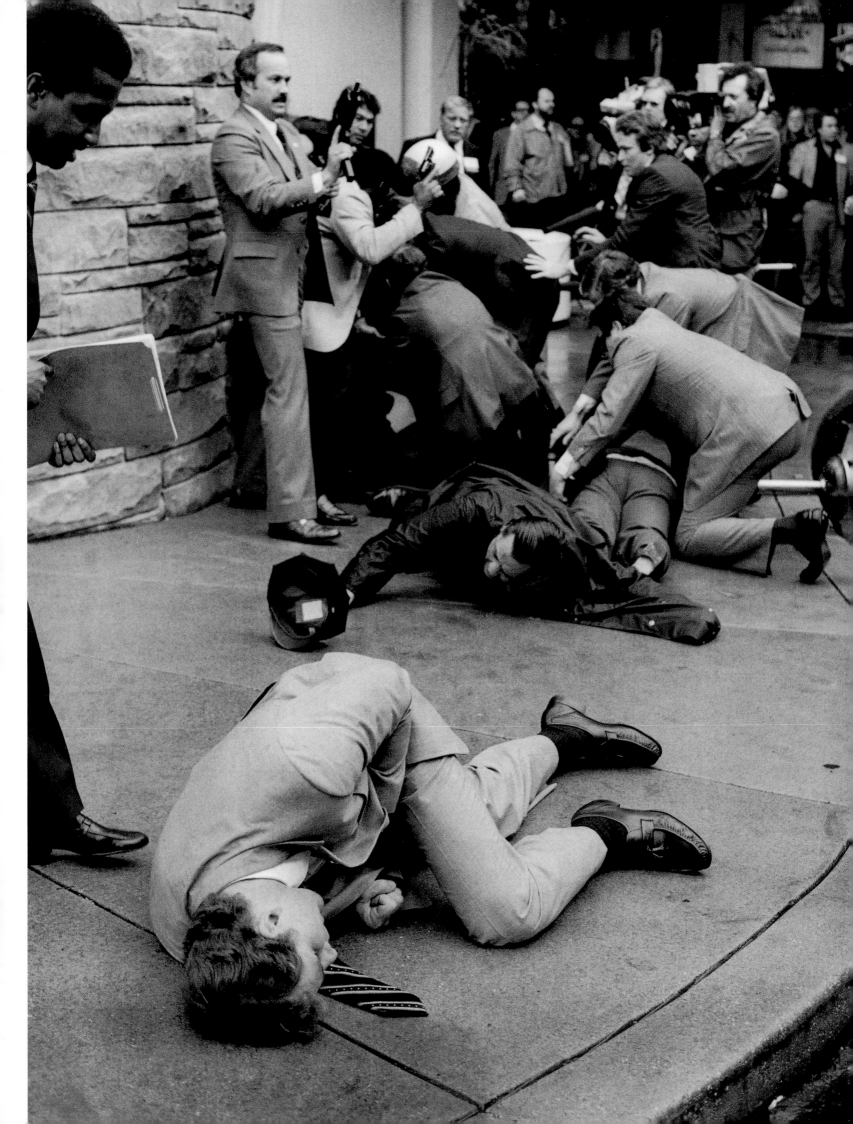

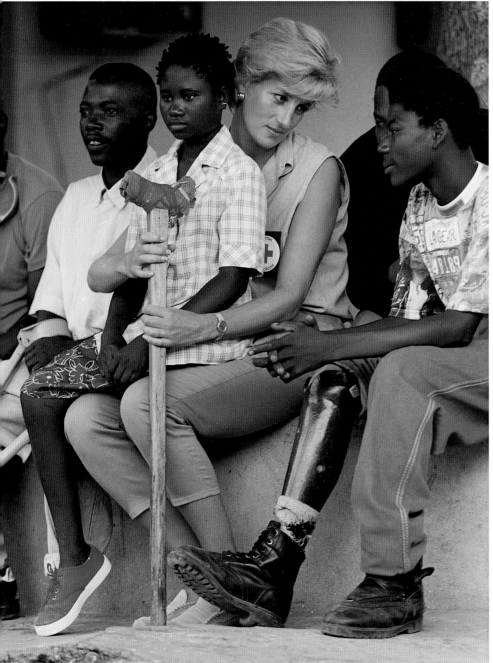

CALCUTTA, INDIA, 1978 – Mother Teresa, head of the Missionaries of Charity, cradles an armless baby girl at her order's orphanage in Calcutta. Mother Teresa rescued the baby from the slums, saving her life.

Eddie Adams

LUANDA, ANGOLA, JAN. 14, 1997 – Britain's Princess Diana talks to amputees at the Neves Bendinha Orthopedic Workshop while visiting Angola in an effort to create awareness about land mines. Sitting on Diana's lap is 13-year-old Sandra Thijica, who lost her left leg to a land mine while working in fields with her mother.

Joao Silva

CALCUTTA, INDIA, SEPT. 9, 1997 – A street urchin, name unknown, waits in line outside St. Thomas' church with a bouquet of flowers to pay last respects to Mother Teresa, winner of the 1979 Nobel Peace Prize for her work with the poor. Thousands of mourners filed past her glass-encased coffin inside the church.

David Longstreath

GULF STREAM, FLA., NOV. 12, 1988 – Waves splash President-elect George Bush as he casts a line surf-fishing shortly after winning the 1988 U.S. election.

Kathy Willens

NEW ENGLAND, MAY 29, 1939 – Former President Herbert Hoover holds a trout while fishing with a guide in New England.

Uncredited

HYDE PARK, N.Y., AUG. 6, 1932 – New York Gov. Franklin D. Roosevelt, Democratic presidential nominee, swims in the pool on his estate.

Uncredited

ASTORIA, ORE., MAY 24, 1968 – U.S. Sen. Robert F. Kennedy runs through the surf with his dog Freckles during a stop on his campaign for the Democratic presidential nomination.

Barry Sweet

STERLING HEIGHTS, MICH., SEPT. 13, 1988 – U.S. Democratic presidential candidate Michael Dukakis gets a ride in a new General Dynamics M1-A-1 battle tank. Dukakis was ridiculed by Republicans, including rival George Bush, who charged that the governor tried to fool voters into thinking he was in favor of increased military spending by "riding around in a tank."

Michael Samojeden

RICHMOND, VA., OCT. 15, 1992 – President George Bush, left, talks with independent presidential candidate Ross Perot, while Democratic candidate Bill Clinton gestures at the conclusion of a televised presidential debate.

Marcy Nighswander
Pulitzer Prize

BETHESDA, MD., OCT. 20, 1965 – During a news
conference at Bethesda Naval Hospital, President Lyndon B. Johnson displays his incision
from gallbladder and kidney stone surgery.

Charles P. Gorry

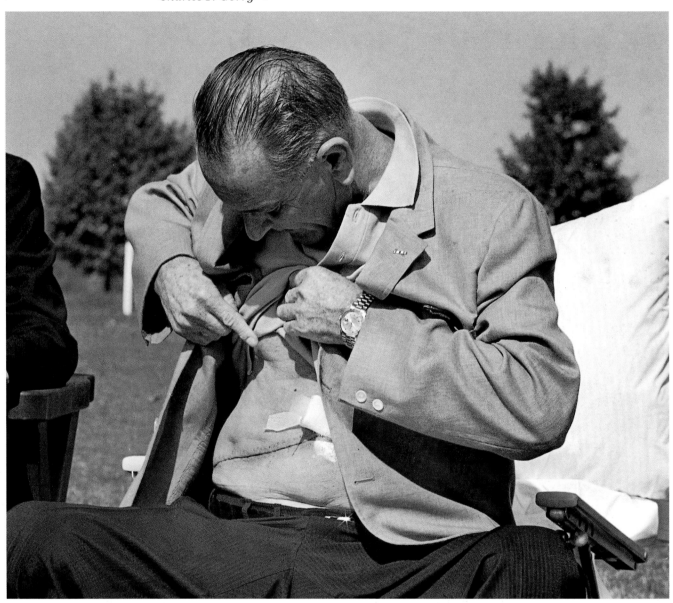

BRUSSELS, BELGIUM, JUNE 26, 1974 – President
Richard M. Nixon checks his watch while shak-
ing hands as he heads to the Royal Palace for a
luncheon with Belgium's King Baudouin.

Charles Tasnadi

CHICAGO, JULY 8, 1952 – Delegates to the
Republican National Convention listen to a
speech by former President Herbert Hoover.
William Smith

BOSTON, APRIL 28, 1992 – Democratic presidential hopeful Bill Clinton addresses the media as U.S. Rep. Joseph Kennedy of Massachusetts looks on during a campaign stop.

Stephan Savoia
Pulitzer Prize

57

STRUGGLE

SPRINGFIELD, COLO., MARCH 25, 1935 – Children covering their faces pump water as soil swept up in windstorms fills the air and destroys thousands of acres of farmland known as the Dust Bowl.

Uncredited

DES MOINES, IOWA, JULY 13, 1993 – Pam Christian lies exhausted on a sandbag dike as residents of central Iowa battle floods that devastated much of the Midwestern United States.

Jeff Beiermann

MONTGOMERY, ALA., FEB. 13, 1945 – Mr. and Mrs. C.M. Levins hold their 3-month-old daughter after crawling from the debris of their home, destroyed by a tornado.

Horace Cort

KOBE, JAPAN, JAN. 20, 1995 – A bicyclist pauses to look at a bus hanging over the edge of an expressway that collapsed in one of Japan's deadliest earthquakes. More than 5,000 people died in the magnitude 7.2 quake.

Eric Draper

(*PREVIOUS PAGES*) **GUAYAMA, PUERTO RICO, SEPT. 10, 1996** – Miguel Ariel Rodriguez, left, and Jose Luis de Leon struggle to rescue 1-year-old Cassandra Gomez from above the raging floodwaters of Hurricane Hortense. Cassandra was saved, but four other family members, including her mother, were lost in the floods.

John McConnico

LAGUNA BEACH, CALIF., OCT. 28, 1993 – A single home sits virtually untouched after Southern California wildfires reduced neighboring homes to rubble.

Douglas C. Pizac

TARLAC, PHILIPPINES, JUNE 22, 1991 – As ash from erupting Mount Pinatubo blocks the mid-day sun, Filipino tribesmen cover their faces and flee villages near the volcano.

Itsuo Inouye

Fort Lauderdale, Fla., July 19, 1935 – The body of 32-year-old Rubin Stacy hangs from a tree as neighbors visit the site. Stacy was lynched by a mob of masked men who seized him from the custody of sheriff's deputies for allegedly attacking a white woman.

Uncredited

BIRMINGHAM, ALA., JULY 15, 1963 – Firefighters
turn hoses full force on civil rights demonstrators.
Bill Hudson

BIRMINGHAM, ALA., MAY 3, 1963 – A police officer and dog attack a demonstrator. Birmingham
was the focus of confrontations over civil rights
in the spring of 1963.

Bill Hudson

WASHINGTON, MAY 20, 1948 – George Gillette, left foreground, chairman of the Fort Berthold Indian Tribal Council, covers his face and weeps as Secretary of the Interior J.A. Krug signs a contract to buy 155,000 acres of North Dakota's best Native American land for a government reservoir.

William Chaplis

TALLAHASSEE, FLA., JUNE 21, 1982 – Women supporters of the Equal Rights Amendment voice their disapproval after the Florida Senate voted 22–16 against the proposed U.S. constitutional amendment.

Ray Fairall

NEW YORK, FEBRUARY 1942 – The former luxury passenger liner *Normandie,* in New York for refitting as the World War II troopship *Lafayette,* lies capsized at her 50th Street pier after a fire during renovations.

Uncredited

BERLIN, JULY 9, 1948 – Youngsters stand on a bomb-damaged building near Tempelhof Airport as a U.S. cargo plane flies overhead after delivering a load of coal. Airlifts broke the Soviet blockade of land routes to Berlin.

Henry Burroughs

BERLIN, Nov. 10, 1989 – Berliners sing and dance on top of the wall in front of the Brandenburg Gate to celebrate the opening of the border between East and West Germany. Thousands of East German citizens crossed into the West after East German authorities opened all border crossings.

Thomas Kienzle

BERLIN, Nov. 12, 1989 – A man hammers at the Berlin Wall as the border barrier between East and West Germany is torn down after 28 years, symbolically ending the Cold War.

John Gaps III

BEIJING, MAY 5, 1989 – A man blocks a line of tanks on Beijing's Changan Boulevard after Chinese forces crushed pro-democracy demonstrations in Tiananmen Square. The man was pulled away by bystanders, and the tanks continued on their way.

Jeff Widener

MOSCOW, AUG. 20, 1991 – A Muscovite applauds a speech by Alexander Yakovlev, former adviser to President Mikhail Gorbachev. Yakovlev denounced the doomed Kremlin coup attempt that briefly drove Gorbachev from office.

Boris Yurchenko
Pulitzer Prize

BANGKOK, THAILAND, OCT. 6, 1976 – A member of a Thai political faction strikes at the lifeless body of a hanged student outside Thammasat University. Police stormed the university after students demanded the expulsion of a former military ruler and barricaded themselves in the school.

Neal Ulevich
Pulitzer Prize

SOWETO, SOUTH AFRICA, SEPT. 15, 1990 – The burning body of a man identified as a Zulu Inkatha supporter is clubbed by followers of the rival African National Congress.

Greg Marinovich
Pulitzer Prize

GAZA CITY, Nov. 25, 1994 – Muslim worshipers bow in prayer outside the overcrowded Palestine Mosque one week after Palestinian police opened fire, killing 13 fundamentalist Muslims. The demonstrators had protested the peace process with Israel.

Jerome Delay

JERUSALEM, Nov. 26, 1995 – Thousands of ultra-Orthodox Jews surround rabbis to protest an archaeological dig that unearthed a 2,000-year-old Jewish burial chamber. Ultra-Orthodox Jews oppose tampering with Jewish graves.

Eyal Warshavsky

81

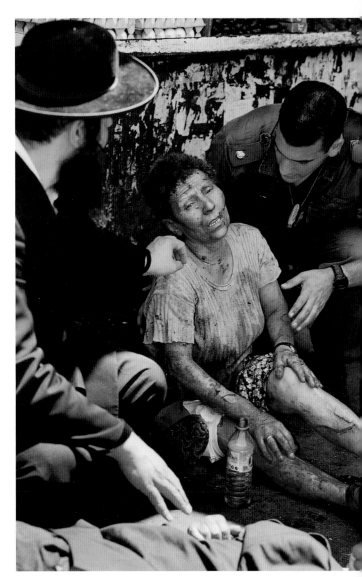

HEBRON, WEST BANK, SEPT. 26, 1995 – An Israeli soldier provides cover from an angry crowd as two other Israeli soldiers detain and drag a Palestinian youth suspected of stone throwing during clashes in the West Bank.

Jerome Delay

JERUSALEM, JULY 30, 1997 – An Orthodox Jew, left, and an Israeli soldier tend to a woman injured in a double bomb blast that killed 13 people and injured more than 150 at Jerusalem's Mahane Yehuda market.

Jacqueline Arzt Larma

PORT-AU-PRINCE, HAITI, SEPT. 18, 1994 – The body of a murdered man lies on a sidewalk near the capital's Roman Catholic Cathedral. Street violence and unrest preceded the arrival of the U.S.-led Multinational Force.

Bebeto Matthews

PORT-AU-PRINCE, HAITI, MARCH 21, 1995 – Gargot Charles, 14, center, measures his sister, Martine, 8, to see how much she has grown, while his mother, Mimose, watches. Gargot helped care for five brothers and sisters in the one-room household so that his mother could earn a living selling water at a market.

Ruth Fremson

MANAURE, COLOMBIA, JULY 10, 1996 – A Wayuu boy wears his father's boots in the salt mines where hundreds of families work during the three-month salt harvest.

Ricardo Mazalan

DEAMY HOLLOW, W.VA., 1969 – Pony driver John Streets pauses outside an independent coal mine where he earns $14.80 per day.

Eddie Adams

Chicago, May 30, 1937 – Police using guns, clubs and tear gas wade into marching strikers outside the Republic Steel plant during protests in the early days of union organization.

Carl Linde

NEW YORK, NOV. 3, 1952 – Police officer Joseph Shavelson holds his gun on James McGrane, one of three suspects in the robbery of a bowling alley on West 50th Street. A second suspect lies wounded on the sidewalk; the third suspect escaped.

Harris Rodvogin

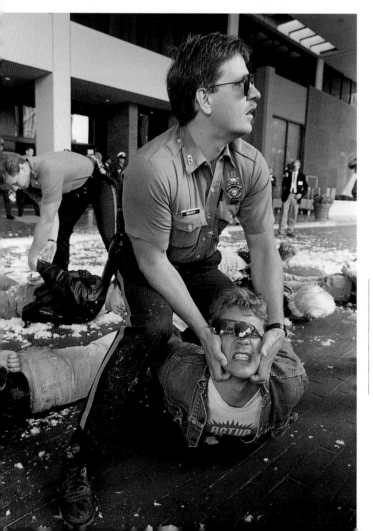

KANSAS CITY, MO., SEPT. 17, 1990 – A police officer holds an AIDS protester in place while waiting for handcuffs to arrive. AIDS activists were demonstrating outside a medical convention, claiming doctors were trying to prevent the use of alternative treatments for the disease.

Cliff Schiappa

BARI, ITALY, AUG. 9, 1991 – Thousands of Albanians fleeing starvation in their impoverished homeland and seeking asylum in Italy crowd the dock after arriving by freighter.

Luca Turi

MEMPHIS, TENN., JAN. 29, 1937 – Mrs. Winifred Waver and her baby son Charles, refugees from flooded Luxora, Ark., wait at a refugee camp for the floodwaters to subside. The tags on her neck provide identification.

James Keen

90

KABUL, AFGHANISTAN, OCT. 6, 1996 – A malaria patient lies in a Kabul hospital with her face covered in accordance with Islamic code that requires a woman to be covered from head to toe in public. The code was enforced after the city's takeover by Islamic Taliban soldiers.

John Moore

BAIDOA, SOMALIA, DEC. 16, 1992 – Aabiba Nuur, who weighs only 46 pounds, sits in a feeding center dedicated to Somali adults in this town devastated by the country's famine and civil war.

Jerome Delay

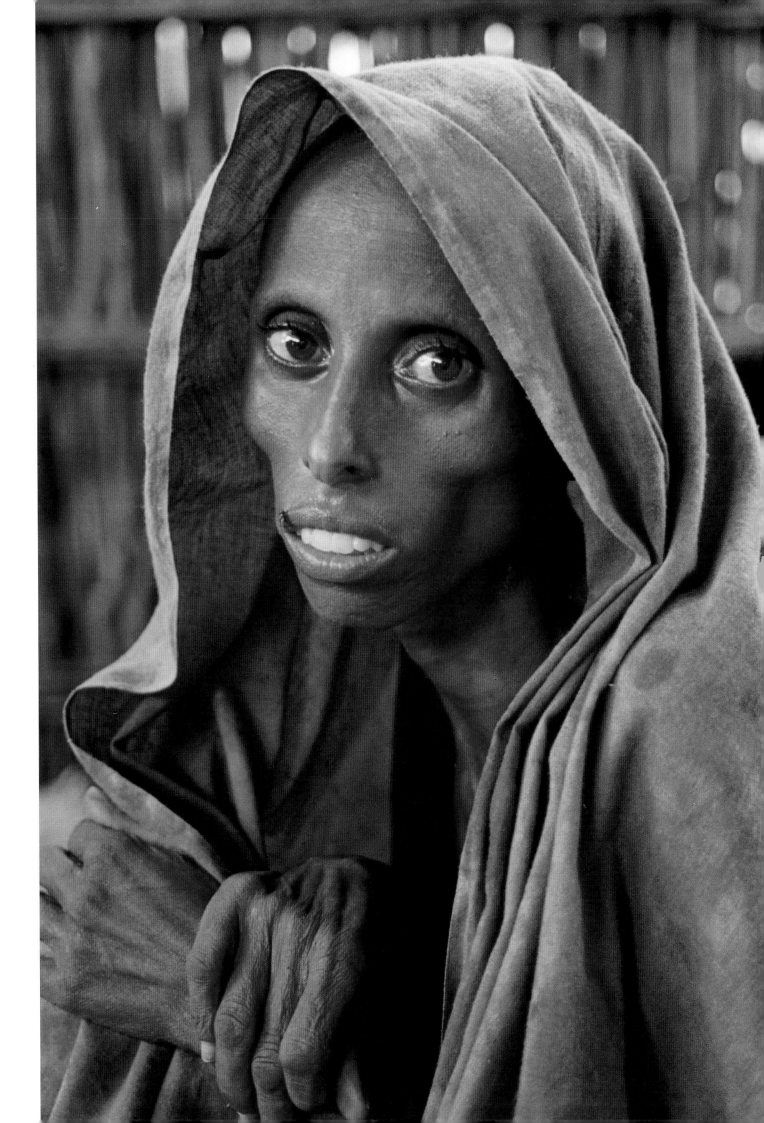

WAR

TRANG BANG, VIETNAM, JUNE 8, 1972 – Phan Thi Kim Phuc, center, her burning clothes torn off, flees with other children after U.S. planes mistakenly dropped napalm on South Vietnamese troops and civilians. Kim Phuc became a symbol of the civilian suffering in the Vietnam War.

Huynh Cong "Nick" Ut
Pulitzer Prize

TORONTO, MAY 25, 1997 – Now a Canadian resident, Kim Phuc plays with her 3-year-old son, Thomas Huy Hoang, at a friend's home.

Huynh Cong "Nick" Ut

CENTRAL HIGHLANDS, VIETNAM, JANUARY 1966 –
First Cavalry Division Medic Thomas Cole of
Richmond, Va., himself wounded, looks up with
one unbandaged eye while treating Staff Sgt.
Harrison Pell during a firefight in the Central
Highlands during the Vietnam War.

Henri Huet

FOSTER CITY, CALIF., MARCH 17, 1973 –
Released prisoner of war Lt. Col. Robert L. Stirm
is greeted by his family at Travis Air Force Base
as he returns home from the Vietnam War.

Sal Veder
Pulitzer Prize

SAIGON, VIETNAM, JUNE 11, 1963 – Quang Duc, a Buddhist monk, burns himself to death on a Saigon street to protest alleged persecution of Buddhists by the South Vietnamese government.
Malcolm Browne

BEIRUT, LEBANON, SEPT. 27, 1982 – A Palestinian woman brandishes helmets during a memorial service for victims of Lebanon's Sabra refugee camp massacre. She claimed the helmets were worn by those who massacred Palestinian men, women and children.

Bill Foley
Pulitzer Prize

INDIAN OCEAN, JANUARY 1942 – An Indian sailor pleads for water from a lifeboat adrift in the Indian Ocean. AP photographer Frank "Pappy" Noel shot this photo from his own lifeboat after a Japanese torpedo sank a ship carrying Noel, the sailors and others from Singapore. Noel and his fellow survivors eventually reached Sumatra.

Frank Noel
Pulitzer Prize

Iwo Jima, Volcano Islands, Feb. 19, 1945 – U.S. Marines hit the beach in the war against Japan, some dragging equipment while others race over the top of a sand dune.

Joe Rosenthal

PARIS, AUG. 29, 1944 – Thousands of American soldiers march along the Champs Elysees after the liberation of Paris during World War II.

Peter J. Carroll

PARIS, DEC. 10, 1949 – A veteran of World War II waves his crutches as he and other disabled French servicemen demonstrate for higher pensions.

Jean-Jacques Levy

JOUY-EN-JOSAS, FRANCE, AUG. 24, 1944 –
Frenchmen kick and jeer German prisoners led
through the town of Jouy-en-Josas, 11 miles from
Paris, one day before the French capital was
liberated.

Dan Grossi

DACCA, BANGLADESH, DEC. 18, 1971 – In newly
independent Bangladesh, a guerrilla leader
beats a victim during the torture and execution
of four men suspected of collaborating with Pak-
istani militiamen accused of murder, rape and
looting during months of civil war.

Horst Faas/Michel Laurent
Pulitzer Prize

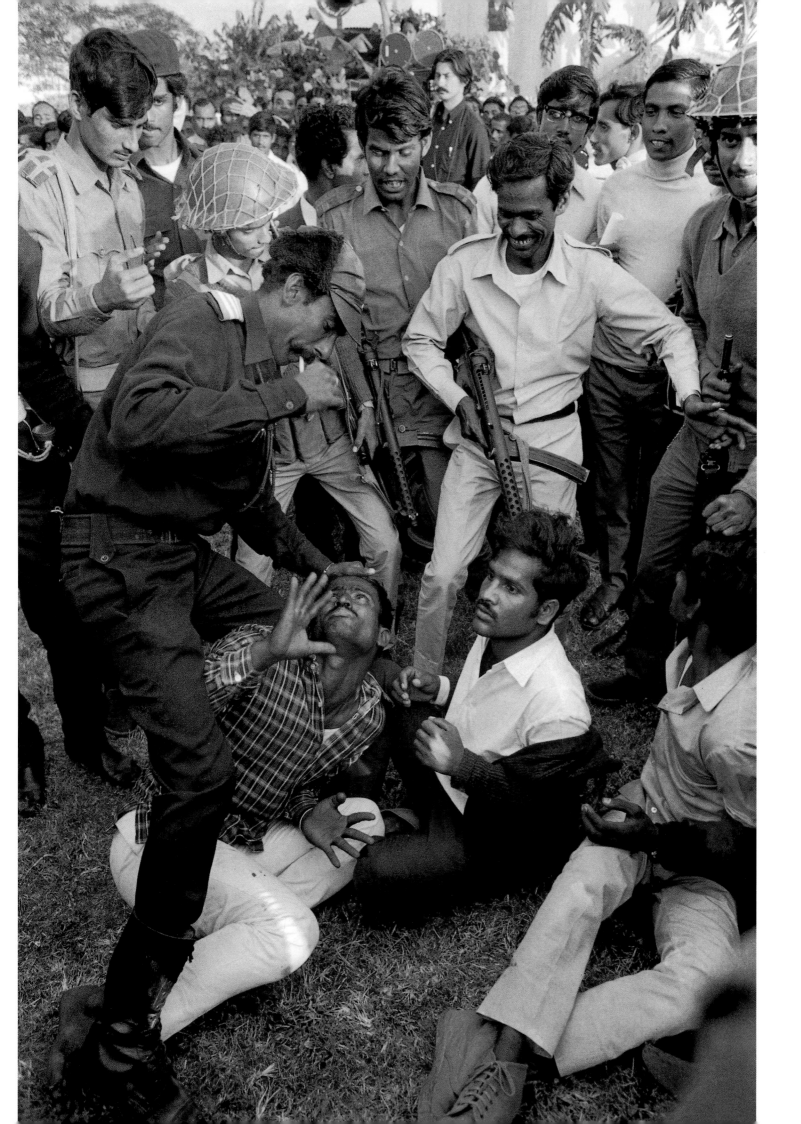

GERMANY, MARCH 26, 1945 – German prisoners who surrendered to U.S. Gen. George Patton's Allied forces march to the Rhine for transport by ferry in the final months of World War II.

Byron Rollins

SAUDI ARABIA, Nov. 4, 1990 – Responding to Iraq's invasion of Kuwait, troops of the U.S. 1st Cavalry Division deploy across the Saudi desert during preparations prior to the Gulf War.

Greg English

PYONGYANG, KOREA, DEC. 4, 1950 – Korean refugees cling to the twisted girders of a bridge spanning the Taedong River as they flee southward from the advance of Chinese Communists in the Korean War.

Max Desfor
Pulitzer Prize

YANGJI, KOREA, JAN. 27, 1951 – A pair of bound hands and a breathing hole in the snow reveal the presence of the body of a Korean civilian shot and left to die by retreating Communists during the Korean War.

Max Desfor

VIETNAM, MARCH 19, 1964 – The body of a child is held by his father as South Vietnamese Army Rangers look down from a tank. The child was killed as government forces pursued Viet Cong guerrillas into a village near the Cambodian border.

Horst Faas
Pulitzer Prize

SARAJEVO, BOSNIA-HERZEGOVINA, NOV. 18, 1994 – Seven-year-old Nermin Divovic, killed by a sniper's bullet, lies in a pool of his own blood as U.N. firefighters rush to his side during war in the former Yugoslavia.

Enric Marti

ON THE RWANDAN BORDER, AUG. 20, 1994 – Rwandan refugee children plead with soldiers to let them cross a bridge into Zaire to rejoin their mothers, who had crossed the bridge moments before the border was closed.

Jean-Marc Bouju
Pulitzer Prize

SARAJEVO, BOSNIA-HERZEGOVINA, NOV. 10, 1992 – A man puts his hands to the window of a bus carrying his son and wife from the besieged city of Sarajevo to safety during the Bosnian War.

Laurent Rebours

NDOSHO, ZAIRE, JULY 28, 1994 – A Rwandan child, too weak to stand in line for a vaccination, rests his head on a ledge at a crowded refugee camp for orphaned children near Goma, Zaire.

Jacqueline Arzt Larma
Pulitzer Prize

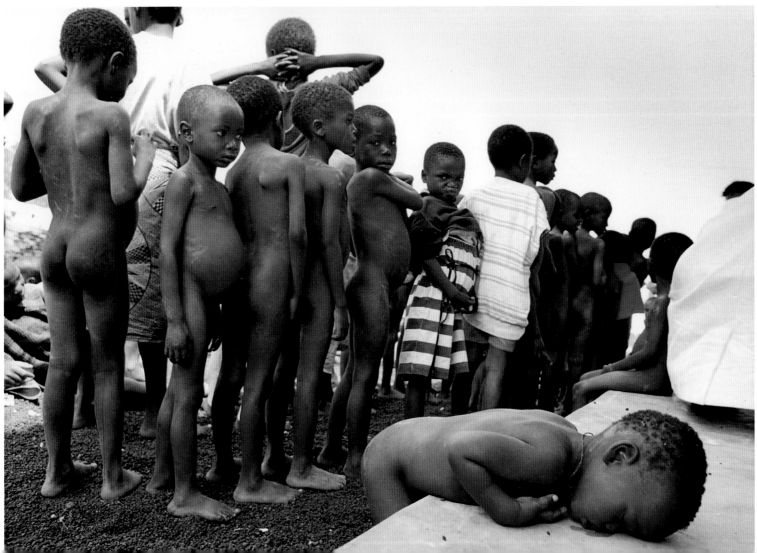

NAZRAN, RUSSIA, FEB. 10, 1995 – Chechen refugee children play on a platform beside the train cars their families call home in Nazran, capital of the Russian republic of Ingushetia.

Olga Shalygin

GROZNY, RUSSIA, JAN. 15, 1995 – Chechens carry a dead peasant woman toward a car minutes after a Russian warplane bombed three farm stables containing cattle southwest of Grozny. Russian and Chechen forces were battling for control of the Chechen capital.

Peter Dejong

119

SASEBO, JAPAN, DEC. 20, 1946 – Japanese soldiers and civilians being returned from China to Japan by U.S. troops at the end of World War II set up temporary shelter in barracks while awaiting transportation home.

Julian Wilson

TRAVNIK, BOSNIA-HERZEGOVINA, NOV. 6, 1992 – Refugees from the Serbian-occupied town of Jajce huddle together at a temporary refugee center during the ethnic war in the former Yugoslavia.

Martin Nangle

SEATTLE, JULY 11, 1969 – A woman is overcome
by emotion as soldiers of the U.S. Army's 3rd
Battalion, 60th Infantry, parade in Seattle. The
troops were among the first ordered home from
the Vietnam War.

Barry Sweet

NEW YORK, JUNE 11, 1991 – After breaking through police lines, Debi Kahn of New Jersey jumps into the arms of a returning Gulf War veteran during New York's Welcome Home Parade.

Doug Mills

NEW YORK, AUG. 31, 1945 – World War II veterans returning from Europe fill every porthole as the *Queen Elizabeth* pulls into a pier in New York harbor.

Uncredited

MOMENTS

WARSAW, POLAND, NOVEMBER 1946 – A portrait photographer uses his own backdrop rather than showing the city's World War II ruins in his photographs.

Michael Nash

CAIRO, EGYPT, MAY 18, 1996 – Illuminated pyramids frame a temporary glass squash court set up on Egypt's Giza Plateau, near Cairo, for an international squash tournament.

Enric Marti

LOS ANGELES, JUNE 1931 – National spring-
board diving champion Georgia Coleman shoots
an arrow, which she says improves her balance
and form, while practicing to defend her title.
Uncredited

ATLANTIC CITY, N.J., SEPT. 16, 1946 – Izzy Weintraub of Atlantic City and Catherine Hollis of Chester, Pa., eat cherrystone clams at the Atlantic City annual clam-eating contest. In 20 minutes they finished 96 and 66 clams respectively.

Sam Meyers

NEW YORK, DEC. 24, 1946 – A Christmas Eve
shopper with a crated rocking horse tries to hail
a cab outside Macy's department store.

Carl Nesensohn

NEW YORK, DEC. 20, 1994 – Sidewalk Santas
come to the aid of bicyclist Philip Anderson, who
was struck by a van. Anderson was hospitalized,
and the Santas went back to promoting a neighborhood business.

Marty Lederhandler

CULVER CITY, CALIF., 1928 – Contestants compete in a marathon dance contest. Marathon dances became fixtures of the 1920s and 1930s.

Uncredited

New York, April 24, 1953 – New Yorkers Lee Moates and Tonita Malau show their winning style during a lindy contest on the block-long floor of Harlem's Savoy Ballroom.

H.V. Nolde

STATE COLLEGE, PA., JUNE 1954 – U.S. Secretary of Agriculture Ezra Taft Benson samples milk directly from a Holstein cow while visiting Pennsylvania State University's farm.

Paul Vathis

PAMPLONA, SPAIN, JULY 7, 1996 – A runner falls in front of a bull during the San Fermin festival's annual running of the bulls.

Santiago Lyon

NEW YORK, 1927 – Aviator Charles A. Lindbergh stands in front of his plane, *The Spirit of St. Louis,* before his historic New York to Paris solo flight.

Uncredited

NEW YORK, SEPT. 21, 1934 – Bronx carpenter Bruno Richard Hauptmann, accused in the kidnapping death of toddler Charles Lindbergh Jr., poses for mugshots in police headquarters. Hauptmann was later convicted and executed.

Uncredited

LONDONDERRY, NORTHERN IRELAND, MAY 22, 1932 – A crowd cheers for Amelia Earhart, the first woman to fly across the Atlantic alone, as she boards her plane in Londonderry for the trip to London.

Uncredited

MEMPHIS, TENN., FEB. 5, 1968 – Entertainer
Elvis Presley and his wife, Priscilla, admire their
newborn baby, Lisa Marie.

Perry Aycock

Pasadena, Calif., Aug. 11, 1943 – Fans surround crooner Frank Sinatra as he arrives for Hollywood film and singing engagements.

John T. Burns

NEW YORK, SEPT. 16, 1964 – The curtain rises on the British rock 'n' roll sensation, the Beatles, at a charity concert.

Uncredited

LAS VEGAS, SEPTEMBER 1970 – Louis Armstrong shares a quiet moment with his trumpet in a Las Vegas dressing room.

Eddie Adams

BEVERLY HILLS, CALIF., JULY 1992 – Computer-
ized hallucinations surround Timothy Leary at
his home. Leary encouraged the use of drugs,
specifically LSD, as a form of enlightenment, and
inspired a broad following.

Mark J. Terrill

ROME, Nov. 2, 1993 – Carabinieri paramilitary police, front, and metropolitan police stand at attention beside the coffin of Italian film director Federico Fellini against a studio backdrop from Fellini's last film.

Massimo Sambucetti

NEW YORK, MAY 24, 1962 – A crowd stands transfixed watching the progress of astronaut Scott Carpenter's triple orbit of the Earth on a giant television screen in Grand Central Terminal.

Robert Kradin

NEW YORK, AUG. 31, 1932 – Eclipse watchers squint through protective film as they view a partial eclipse of the sun from the top deck of the Empire State Building.

Uncredited

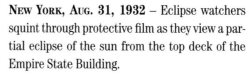

(*PREVIOUS PAGES*) SALISBURY PLAIN, ENGLAND, MARCH 28, 1997 – Comet Hale-Bopp streaks across the night sky above the ancient stone circle of Stonehenge in southwest England.

Alastair Grant

NEW YORK, JULY 4, 1961 – Two visitors to New York's Coney Island ride the Parachute Drop high above sunbathers on the beach.

Uncredited

WASHINGTON, JUNE 28, 1994 – Italian goalie Luca Marchegiani lies on the field as a goal by Mexico's Marcelino Bernal hits the net during World Cup matches at Robert F. Kennedy Stadium. The teams tied 1–1 and both advanced to the next round.

Doug Mills

WIMBLEDON, ENGLAND, JULY 5, 1986 – Martina Navratilova throws back her head in delight as she defeats Hana Mandlikova for her fifth consecutive Wimbledon Tennis Championship.

Dave Caulkin

LEWISTON, MAINE, MAY 25, 1965 – Heavyweight champion Cassius Clay taunts challenger Sonny Liston after dropping him with a right to the jaw in the first round of their fight. Clay was declared the winner.

John Rooney

CHICAGO, AUG. 4, 1950 – Babe Didrikson
Zaharias urges the ball into the cup on the 18th
green of the Tam O'Shanter Country Club in the
Women's All-American Golf Tournament.

Ed Maloney

NORTH PLAINS, ORE., AUG. 25, 1996 – Golfer Tiger Woods throws up his arm in jubilation as he ties for the lead after 35 holes of the U.S. Amateur Championship. Woods won the title on the 38th hole.

Jack Smith

KANSAS CITY, MO., SEPT. 29, 1993 – Kansas City Royals baseball player George Brett kisses home plate at Kauffman Stadium after the last home game of his career. Brett got an eighth-inning hit that tied the game as the Royals went on to beat the Cleveland Indians 3–2.

Cliff Schiappa

EZEIZA, ARGENTINA, MARCH 13, 1995 – Mexico's catcher, Alberto Vargas, tries unsuccessfully to blow a ball into foul territory in a game against Guatemala during the Pan American Games. The ball was ruled fair by the umpire.

Joe Cavaretta

PHILADELPHIA, JAN. 27, 1985 – John McEnroe kicks back a television camera that he felt was crowding him on the court during the finals of the U.S. Pro Indoor Tennis Championships. McEnroe defeated Czechoslovakian Miloslav Mecir to win the tournament.

Amy Sancetta

HAMAR, NORWAY, FEB. 25, 1994 – U.S. figure skater Tonya Harding shows to judges what she claims is a faulty skate as she appeals for a chance to restart her free-skating program at the Winter Olympic Games.

Jack Smith

BERLIN, AUG. 8, 1936 – Jesse Owens of the United States wears the winner's oak leaf crown after winning the broad jump, becoming the first athlete to win four gold medals at a single Olympic Games. On the right is runner-up Carl Ludwig Long of Germany, saluting Nazi leader Adolf Hitler, and on the left is Naoto Tajima of Japan, who placed third.

Anthony Camerano

MEXICO CITY, OCT. 16, 1968 – Extending gloved hands skyward to protest racial inequality, U.S. athletes Tommie Smith, center, and John Carlos stare downward as the American national anthem is played during award ceremonies for the 200-meter run at the Olympic Games. Australian silver medalist Peter Norman is at left. After Smith and Carlos were suspended for their actions, former Olympic gold medalist Jesse Owens intervened to prevent a walkout protest by U.S. black athletes.

Uncredited

MONTREAL, JULY 1976 – Nadia Comaneci of Romania dismounts from the uneven parallel bars during a perfect "10" performance at the Summer Olympic Games. It was the first time in Olympic history that a gymnast scored perfect marks.

Uncredited

BARCELONA, SPAIN, JULY 27, 1992 – China's Fu Mingxia arches her back in midair during the women's 10-meter diving competition at the Summer Olympic Games. The 13-year-old took the gold medal in the event.

Santiago Lyon

BARCELONA, SPAIN, AUG. 7, 1992 – U.S. long jumper Carl Lewis makes his third jump of the Olympic finals, beating world record holder Mike Powell to become the first three-time gold medalist in the long jump. Lewis won a fourth gold medal in the long jump in 1996.

Eric Risberg

MIAMI, JAN. 12, 1969 – Six-foot-7-inch Baltimore Colt defensive end Bubba Smith towers over New York Jets quarterback Joe Namath, but is unable to prevent Namath from making a pass during Super Bowl III. Namath completed 17 of 28 passes for 206 yards, leading the Jets to a 16–7 upset victory over the Colts.

Uncredited

SAN JOSE, CALIF., JUNE 5, 1993 – An unidentified boy tries to push Salevaa Atisance, who goes by the sumo name of Konishiki, during opening ceremonies of a sumo wrestling tournament. Konishiki weighs 576 pounds.

Paul Sakuma

INDIANAPOLIS, MAY 28, 1995 – Moments after the start of the Indy 500, Stan Fox's car strikes the outside wall of the Indianapolis Motor Speedway. Still strapped in the wreckage, his feet and legs exposed, Fox hurtles backward over the cars of Paul Tracy, left, and Eddie Cheever. Fox suffered serious head injuries in the crash, but survived.

Jim Stewart

PITTSBURGH, SEPT. 20, 1964 – New York Giants quarterback Y.A. Tittle kneels dazed and bleeding on the field after being hit and intercepted for a touchdown by the Pittsburgh Steelers.

Dozier Mobley

NEW YORK, AUG. 21, 1942 – Baseball Hall of
Fame star Babe Ruth warms up at Yankee Sta-
dium for an exhibition to raise money for the
Army-Navy Relief Fund during World War II.

Tom Sande

PHOENIX, JUNE 20, 1993 – Chicago Bulls star Michael Jordan celebrates after the Bulls beat the Phoenix Suns by one point to win their third consecutive National Basketball Association championship.

John Swart

NEW YORK, 1915 – An AP teletype operator uses an early teletype model to transmit a news story. The introduction of the teletype in 1914 allowed the AP to switch from sending news by telegraph to transmitting from a keyboard connected to distant printers in a 60-words-per-minute web that eventually covered the world. In the 1970s news moved at 1,500 words per minute. By the late 1980s, news traveled by satellite at 12,000 words per minute.

THE STORY OF THE ASSOCIATED PRESS

By Charles J. Hanley
Associated Press Special Correspondent

The Associated Press came to life 150 years ago in the stuttering tap of a telegraph key. That thin stream of dots and dashes, an electric hum across a young American countryside, never stopped. It has grown into a river.

Today it flows through space, in bursts of bits and bytes relayed by satellite to newspapers, radio and television stations, computer screens across the nation and around the globe, a river of words and pictures that is the greatest single source of news about the world for the world.

That world changes fast, and so has the AP. But a century and a half later, the organization's founders would recognize today's underlying mission: to report the news accurately, fairly and efficiently.

Or as an early AP correspondent, Lawrence A. Gobright, put it: "My business is to communicate facts."

The facts communicated have often been the facts that defined history.

It was an AP reporter who saved Lincoln's words at Gettysburg for posterity, and the AP office in San Francisco that kept the nation informed after the 1906 earthquake. It was an AP photographer who captured forever the sight of Marines raising the flag over Iwo Jima, and another who caught President Reagan in the grim freeze-frames of attempted assassination. It was an AP trio, when Saigon fell, who stayed behind to report it, despite orders from headquarters that they leave.

The unrivaled reach of the world's largest news organization was enough to impress one of the 20th century's least impressionable figures.

Independence leader Mohandas K. Gandhi, freed from prison and dropped off at a remote spot in India in the 1930s, looked up and saw a lone figure approaching in the darkness. It was the AP's Jim Mills.

"I suppose when I go to the Hereafter and stand at the Golden Gate," the disbelieving Gandhi said, "the first person I shall meet will be a correspondent of The Associated Press."

Being there, bearing witness comes at a cost, sometimes in lives.

Mark Kellogg was the first AP correspondent to fall, riding with George Armstrong Custer and the 7th Cavalry to their deaths at the Little Bighorn in 1876. Since then, 22 others have lost their lives in service to the

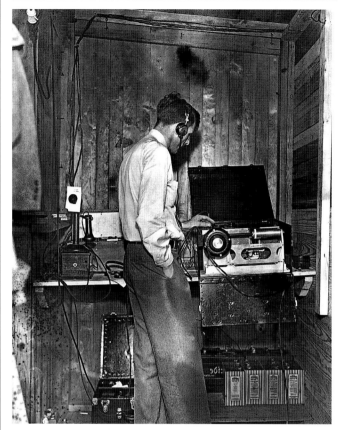

LOUISVILLE, KY., 1936 – Chief Engineer Harold Carlson checks the Wirephoto machine at the 1936 Kentucky Derby, a year after the AP launched the world's first network to transmit pictures by wire. Wirephoto allowed newspapers to print pictures from afar side by side with the news, rather than wait two to four days for mailed photographs.

AP and the news. And still others have sacrificed years to cruel confinement by wartime enemies, by Lebanese hostage-takers, by an Iron Curtain police state.

But as telegraph keys have given way to clattering teletypes, and teletypes to laptops and satellite phones, the AP journalist's drive to be there, to see, to report has never fadēd, despite the dangers and difficulties.

It's an enthusiasm that may have been distilled best in a note sent back to AP headquarters in 1966 by veteran foreign correspondent Hugh A. Mulligan as he journeyed to a new assignment:

"Soon I will be in Vietnam again. Another adventure awaits. . . . I am engaged in the most exciting profession in the world. I have already seen more sights from better seats than any rich man can afford."

The show, for the most part, is not history-making. More than a steady diet of great mo-

ments, the round-the-clock AP "report" offers a menu of everyday events—of weather and news conferences, of stock prices and car pileups three counties away. The AP will cover terrorism in the Mideast, but it's also there to cover high school basketball in the U.S. Midwest.

Doing that takes teamwork, not only among the 3,500 reporters, photographers, newscasters, editors, technicians and other employees of the AP, but also among America's newspapers and broadcasters—the owners, benefactors and beneficiaries of this not-for-profit cooperative.

News from 236 AP bureaus around the nation and the world flows to thousands of news outlets globally, including 99 percent of U.S. dailies and 6,000 U.S. broadcasters, the cooperative's members. In turn, those AP members send news from their localities to the cooperative, supplying raw material for the state-level AP news report.

If staff and members are two pillars of the AP structure, technology is the third.

Since its earliest days, the news service has chased after speed—the quickest route, the best equipment, the latest innovation.

It was the first organization, in 1899, to try out Guglielmo Marconi's new "wireless" device to transmit news. A generation later, it pioneered in sending news photos over the wire. In the 1970s, it plunged into the digital age in a big way. Now a 700-word story that once took 10 minutes to send takes just five seconds.

CLEVELAND, 1936 – Writers and photographers work in the AP's designated space in the press area at the 1936 Republican National Convention.

RED JACKET, W.VA., AUG. 10, 1938 – Pittsburgh photographer Bill Allen creates a temporary darkroom by using the trunk of his car to develop film of a mine explosion in rural West Virginia. AP photographers were adept at setting up darkrooms in virtually any location. That became less necessary with the increased use of filmless digital cameras, introduced in the 1990s.

The AP has the world's most comprehensive photo service, two radio networks, a young, fast-growing video news service, and a central role as a news source on the Internet's World Wide Web.

It has more people in more places covering more stories than anyone. That stuttering stream of 150 years ago has swelled into an estimated 20 million words a day of information.

But bigger and faster is not necessarily better. More words mean more challenges to AP credibility, more weight on the keystone of the structure.

The big blunders become part of agency lore: the false report in 1961 that U.N. Secretary-General Dag Hammarskjold had landed safely at an African airport, when in fact his plane had crashed and he was dead; the misreported "death" of civil rights activist James Meredith, shot and wounded on a Mississippi highway in 1966.

But the rare letdowns serve mostly to point up the record of dependability, and to underline the cautionary commandment that guides the AP's daily work. It's a credo reduced to a few irreducible words by the man leading the news service in its sesquicentennial year.

"We go when we know. And not before," said AP President Louis D. Boccardi.

The AP brand of credibility underpins much of journalism. In fact, standards of objectivity, balance, believability taken for granted today in American news reporting were, in a real sense, given life with the AP.

Not that the 10 men gathered at the New York *Sun* one May day in 1848 had such ideals uppermost in their minds. Their concerns were more down-to-earth.

Revolutions were remaking Europe, the anti-slavery movement was building at home and a presidential campaign was in the offing. Americans' appetite for news was growing, and Sam Morse's new device, the telegraph, had finally broken down age-old barriers of distance.

But the cost of collecting news through the bottlenecked wires of the telegraph companies was proving exorbitant for New York's newspapers.

David Hale, of the *Journal of Commerce,* had a proposal: pool their resources to produce a single telegraphic report on each news event, one they all could publish.

Those listening to him, representatives of five other New York dailies, were veterans of a highly competitive newspaper market. They included the *Herald*'s James Gordon Bennett, the *Tribune*'s Horace Greeley, and Henry Raymond, who later founded *The New York Times.*

They were skeptical but they heard Hale out, and that very day they formed their cooperative,

LOUISVILLE, KY., FEB. 1, 1937 – AP writers and editors work by candlelight after major flooding in the Ohio and Mississippi valleys knocked out power and left thousands of people homeless.

173

NEW YORK, MARCH 1939 – AP motorcycle messenger Pete Schivilla departs with a photo package destined for one of New York City's daily newspapers. Although the AP at that time transmitted photos via Wirephoto, competitive big-city dailies also wanted prints.

not out of any sense of public service or with any intent to invite in others, but simply because the dollar-and-cents logic proved indisputable.

It was the beginning. They called it The Associated Press.

The AP partners, longtime rivals in collecting news from inbound ships off New York, quickly arranged for a steamboat out of Halifax, Nova Scotia, to meet ships from Europe, gather what news they had and rush it to Boston and the telegraph link to New York. Next, the AP's new general agent, Dr. Alexander Jones, signed on telegraph correspondents in key U.S. cities. Soon, the six papers were receiving a regular flow of AP news from beyond New York.

Those reports had an unusual slant to them—no slant at all. In a city and country where newspapers had grown up as partisan, opinionated organs, the AP correspondents had to follow a neutral line, of unadorned fact, to appeal to all their sponsors.

"I do not act as a politician belonging to any school," Gobright pointed out a few years later, "but try to be truthful and impartial."

The 1848 presidential vote was the first big story. Telegraph offices stayed open all night, and Jones worked 72 hours straight—first in a long line of sleep-deprived AP reporters and editors.

The cooperative began selling its news to papers in Philadelphia, Baltimore and other cities, not as members, but as subscribers. The Philadelphia Associated Press, the Western AP and other regional newspaper alliances formed to buy news from the New York AP, provider of national and foreign news.

It was a boom time for newspapers. The newly invented rotary press, replacing flatbed printing, produced bigger, faster editions. And in 1858 news gathering took a big step, across the Atlantic.

The first transoceanic cable was laid, and the first news message from Europe arrived, addressed to The Associated Press, 42 words summarizing five stories in headline form and concluding, "MUTINY BEING QUELLED, ALL INDIA BECOMING TRANQUIL."

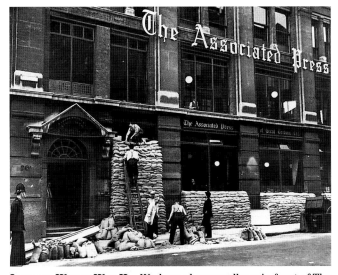

LONDON, WORLD WAR II – Workers place sandbags in front of The Associated Press House at the outbreak of World War II. The five-story building, which housed London AP's news and photo operations, was later hit and damaged during a German air raid.

Soon, it was the tranquillity of America itself that was in question. When hostilities broke out between North and South in 1861, the AP's resourceful chief executive, Daniel Craig, sent out platoons of reporters to learn, on the job, how to cover a war.

Over time, on the move with Union armies, wiring in terse dispatches and fleshing them out with reports sent by messenger, the AP men established a standard for the new specialty of combat correspondent—all under the anony-

IWO JIMA, VOLCANO ISLANDS, FEBRUARY 1945 – AP photographer Joe Rosenthal, left, and Bob Campbell, a U.S. Marine from San Francisco, rest at the base of Mount Suribachi in front of a Japanese gun knocked out during the invasion of the Pacific island. Rosenthal's photograph of the flag raising atop Mount Suribachi won a 1945 Pulitzer Prize and became the emblem of American victory and one of the most famous pictures of all time.

mous byline "From the Associated Press Agent."

Far behind the lines, too, the AP proved its indispensability.

When Abraham Lincoln dedicated the cemetery at Gettysburg in November 1863, the AP's Joseph L. Gilbert faithfully took down the president's words, checking them later against Lincoln's own text. For historians, that AP text became the most reliable account of one of history's most memorable three minutes.

After the war, the reunited nation pushed its horizons westward, and the AP followed. At the same time, the news service sent its first correspondent east, to Europe.

The flow of news widened, outgrowing Western Union's commercial wires, and in 1875 the AP took the big step of leasing its own telegraph wire, a 226-mile line between New York and Washington.

Necessity gave birth to other innovations as well.

For decades, correspondents had written in a slow narrative style. Gobright's wrap-up story the night of Lincoln's assassination, for example, began, "President Lincoln and wife, with other friends, this evening visited Ford's Theatre. . . ."

Not until 200 words later did the reader learn the president had been shot.

But telegraph wires, strung through trees and over fences, were notoriously unreliable. At 30 to 40 words a minute, slow-moving copy often broke off before reaching the real news.

In the 1880s, AP editors began encouraging correspondents to write in a different style: the key facts first, in the "lead" paragraphs, followed by descending layers of detail.

Though born of necessity, this technique of leaving the least for last appealed to readers pressed for time and editors pressed for space. The "inverted pyramid" style championed by the AP became a hallmark of modern journalism.

COLDITZ, GERMANY, SPRING 1945 – AP war correspondent Don Whitehead interviews an American soldier in this embattled German town near Leipzig, where a 17th-century castle served as a Nazi war prison. Whitehead went on to win two Pulitzer Prizes for reporting during the Korean War.

Even as it advanced journalistically, however, the AP remained weak as an organization. Still owned by a handful of New York newspapers, it was viewed as undemocratic by client papers across the country and was resented for demanding what they considered too high a price for its news.

The conflict came to a scandalous head in 1891, when it was learned that some top executives of the New York group had profited from financial stakes in an upstart rival agency they were secretly feeding AP news.

The Western Associated Press led a revolt of

Frank Filan

LOS ANGELES, JUNE 2, 1950 – AP Hollywood columnist Bob Thomas tags along with actress Lucille Ball, who was preparing to star as a door-to-door saleswoman in her next movie and visited a residential neighborhood to get a feel for the job. Thomas went along to get housewife reaction, but there was none—no one recognized either the actress or the columnist.

---

regional associations against New York, reorganizing as a new collective based in Chicago. The old AP soon collapsed, and in 1900 the new one relocated and incorporated in New York as a true, not-for-profit cooperative.

The AP began the new century as a nationally based organization under a forceful general manager, *Chicago Daily News* founder Melville E. Stone. It was now in a strong position to stay ahead of fast-moving times.

An electric typesetting device, the Linotype, was speeding up newspaper production. Telephones had spread everywhere. For the AP, the turning point came in 1914, when the teletype, transmitting words by wire from keyboard to distant printers, was introduced.

It would take years, but eventually the efficient, 60-words-a-minute teletype web covered the country and finally silenced the buzz of dots and dashes. Many small dailies, meanwhile,

began to rely on the telephone, receiving news summaries dictated over the line to several papers at once by AP editors. It was fancifully named the "pony wire," for the old pony express.

That was behind the scenes. On the nation's front pages, the AP was omnipresent, the reliable chronicler of an ever-shrinking nation and world—at times, sometimes critical times, the only chronicler.

When catastrophe befell San Francisco one spring dawn in 1906, the city fell mute as well. Telegraph and telephone wires were broken.

Copy in hand, local AP correspondents dashed from their shattered office to the telegraph company to the cable office, with no luck. Finally a Western Union telegrapher coaxed a line to Chicago back to life briefly, and the AP bulletin went out:

SAN FRANCISCO, APRIL 18—SAN FRANCISCO WAS SHAKEN BY AN EARTHQUAKE AT 5:15 THIS MORNING.

They were the first of 21,300 words transmitted over 24 hours by the San Francisco AP, whose staff ferried back and forth across the bay to Oakland and a wire office. That day and night, the AP alone kept the nation informed of its great American tragedy.

MUNSAN, KOREA, MAY 15, 1953 – Three AP staff members covering the Korean War take a break outside the Munsan bureau—actually the press tent—of "The World's Greatest Newsgathering Organization." Pictured from left to right are correspondents George McArthur and Bill Waugh and photographer Max Desfor. Desfor won the Pulitzer Prize in 1951 for a picture of fleeing Korean War refugees.

Tragedies at sea presented other challenges. After the British liner *Titanic* hit an iceberg and sank off Newfoundland in April 1912, AP shipping news reporter Dick Lee went out to meet survivors aboard the incoming *Carpathia* and pieced together a detailed narrative of the disaster. More than that, Lee arranged for two survivors to write harrowing first-person accounts for the AP wire.

LOS ANGELES, JULY 1960 – AP photographer Harry Harris, left, gestures as he speaks to John F. Kennedy, Adlai Stevenson and Lyndon Johnson, all presidential aspirants, at the Democratic National Convention. Kennedy was nominated for president and later won the election.

It was an era packed with popular, enterprising journalism. But the AP also worked hard at the nuts and bolts of news, especially in developing the news "cooperative."

In 1916, the AP and member newspapers for the first time combined resources to cover a national election, the presidential race between President Woodrow Wilson and Republican Charles Evans Hughes.

Tediously tallying votes on a precinct-by-precinct, county-by-county basis, the AP remained silent as newspapers nationwide rushed their own reports to print declaring Hughes, as expected, the winner.

But late Thursday, two days after the election, a New York AP editor phoned the hotel suite of "President-elect" Hughes and passed on the news: "Tell him he isn't president-elect anymore."

A careful, patient AP had finally filed the bulletin: Wilson had narrowly won California and reclaimed the White House.

"We go when we know." The AP admonition was followed even more famously two years later, in the final hours of World War I.

At midday on Nov. 7, 1918, the United Press—an 11-year-old, profit-making rival to the AP—flashed across its wires word that an armistice had been signed. Church bells rang across the nation. Telephones rang at AP headquarters.

Where was the AP report? Was the big wire service pro-German, or incompetent?

The AP's editors transmitted a note to members saying they had no such announcement. But the pressure built. Newspapers threatened to cancel the service. At one point, angry demonstrators converged on the AP building in New

ATHENS, GA., JAN. 11, 1961 – AP Atlanta newswoman Kathryn Johnson, left, dressed like a student in bobby socks and a sweater to get past officials at the University of Georgia so she could interview the school's first black woman student. The student is 18-year-old Charlayne Hunter, who later became a respected newswoman in her own right as Charlayne Hunter-Gault.

York and were held back by police.

Finally, in midafternoon, the State Department spoke: No armistice had been concluded. Four days later, the real celebrations began, after the AP flashed, "ARMISTICE SIGNED."

In the heady, prosperous years that followed, the "Roaring '20s," speakeasies and gangsters, boxing heroes and movie stars, daredevil aviators and Wall Street speculators were splashed across America's front pages. Reporters had fun, too.

KARACHI, PAKISTAN, 1962 – AP White House reporter Frances Lewine chats with Jacqueline Kennedy on the lawn of the governor's residence in Karachi during the first lady's world tour.

"We were a wild, boisterous, cynical, unmannerly crew," said Lorena Hickok, one of the AP's first woman reporters. "Only the bootleggers loved us."

The AP found a leader for the times—Kent Cooper, a canny, songwriting innovator from Indiana who took charge in 1925 and set about putting more human-interest copy and interviews on the wire, turning Hollywood and science into regular beats, and even encouraging bylines for writers, a break with the anonymous past.

The young sports department came up with a

SAIGON, VIETNAM, MAY 3, 1966 – Two AP Pulitzer Prize winners congratulate AP's Peter Arnett, center, on winning the 1966 Pulitzer for international reporting for coverage of the Vietnam War. Malcolm Browne, left, won the 1964 Pulitzer Prize for reporting from Vietnam, and Horst Faas, right, won the 1965 Pulitzer Prize for photography. Faas also won the 1972 Pulitzer Prize with AP's Michel Laurent for pictures of tortures and executions in Bangladesh.

"Top 10" ranking of college football teams, and an annual AP "All-America" squad—national institutions today.

The expanding news staff, meanwhile, continued to set a standard for "being there."

When Sacco and Vanzetti, convicted of murder in a politically explosive trial, were electrocuted outside Boston in 1927, the AP's W.E. Playfair was the lone reporter to witness the Italian radicals' deaths.

"I am an innocent man," his report quoted a calm Vanzetti as saying moments before execution. "I wish to forgive some people for what they are now doing to me."

And after America's most celebrated baby vanished from his New Jersey home one night in 1932, the AP's Frank Jamieson got a grim exclusive—straight from the governor.

"The stolen baby son of Col. Charles A. Lindbergh was found dead today in the stubbly Sourland hills of New Jersey," Jamieson's dispatch began. His coverage won him a Pulitzer Prize.

The race for news was growing more crowded. The press was still king, but a new medium had entered the field.

INDIANAPOLIS, MAY 1973 – AP sportswriter Karol Stonger sits under the back end of a racing car at the Indianapolis 500 as she interviews a member of driver Mario Andretti's pit crew. Stonger was one of the first women sportswriters for the AP.

The AP had long familiarity with radio. In 1899, it was the first news operation to use Guglielmo Marconi's rudimentary invention as a news-gathering tool, receiving wireless reports on the America's Cup yacht race from offshore. In 1920, in the first "newscast," pioneer station KDKA in Pittsburgh aired results of the Harding-Cox presidential election using AP copy supplied—with AP permission—by the *Pittsburgh Post.*

But newspapers viewed radio as a threat, and a lasting AP link with broadcasting had to wait many years. Photos, on the other hand, couldn't wait.

Cooper inaugurated the service in 1927, distributing news photographs by messenger or mail. And within a few years, with AP money, Bell Laboratories engineered a revolution—an over-the-wire transmission device for images.

The Wirephoto network was switched on early on the morning of Jan. 1, 1935, its first offering an aerial shot of the crash site of a small plane in upstate New York.

Some AP board members had balked at Wirephoto's $5 million development cost, in the midst of a Depression in which AP employees' salaries were cut 10 percent. But Cooper was determined to keep the cooperative in the news industry's front ranks.

His next success: winning board approval in 1937 to move the headquarters from the latest in a series of cramped New York homes into what he called the "dignified showmanship" of Rockefeller Center, the city's spectacular new office complex.

For the rest of the century, the vast fourth-floor newsroom at 50 Rockefeller Plaza would be the worldwide organization's nerve center.

The pneumatic tubes, rumbling teletypes and cigarette-strewn floors eventually made way for the beep of computers and a quieter, smoke-free setting. But the spirit of "being there" never changed, a spirit embodied best in the almost 200 reporters and photographers who fanned out around the globe to cover World War II.

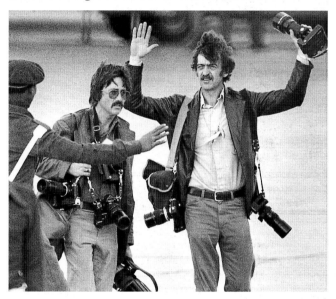

CAIRO, EGYPT, 1979 – AP Washington photographer Bob Daugherty, right, raises his arms ready to be frisked by Egyptian military security during a state visit to Egypt by U.S. President Jimmy Carter. At left is UPI photographer Darryl Heikes.

Five lost their lives. Seven others won Pulitzer Prizes, including Larry Allen, who had eight warships sunk beneath him by the enemy and was rescued each time; Hal Boyle, whose taut tales of the American fighting man moved millions of readers back home; and Joe Rosenthal, who clambered up Iwo Jima's Mount Suribachi to take the flag-raising photo that became the emblem of American victory and one of the most famous pictures of all time.

Inevitably, among thousands of transmissions from dozens of war fronts, error crept in, most

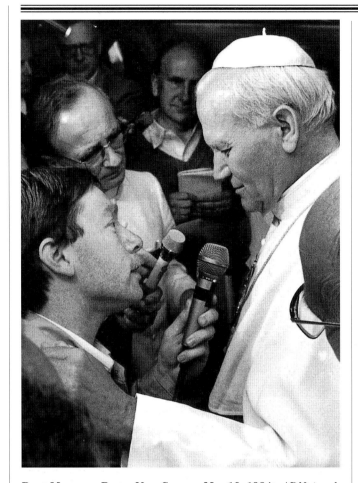

Port Moresby, Papua New Guinea, May 10, 1984 – AP Network News European correspondent Brad Kalbfeld interviews Pope John Paul II on board the pope's plane as it departs New Guinea for Thailand. Kalbfeld filed live AP radio newscasts, special voice reports for radio and television stations and wire stories for newspapers throughout the pope's tour of Asia.

notoriously in the lead-up to D-Day, when a teletype operator at London AP inadvertently transmitted a "practice" flash falsely announcing the invasion of France.

"In news, it's the mistakes that really hurt," Wes Gallagher, leader of AP's D-Day reporters, later reflected.

But mistakes stood out for their rarity, and the news service's coverage of the war set a new standard for courageous, comprehensive reporting on a challenging story, reporting that climaxed on the most controversial of notes.

Early on May 7, 1945, the AP's Ed Kennedy and 16 other correspondents witnessed the signing of the German surrender at Reims, France. This "pool" had pledged to hold the news until the military released it. But German radio then announced the war's end, and Kennedy learned that

the official release would be delayed for political reasons, not for military security.

He filed his flash, and touched off a furor in the U.S. news industry.

Denounced by other journalists as a violator of trust and finding halfhearted support at New York headquarters, Kennedy left the AP. But many colleagues said they would have done the same thing, and ordinary readers sensed that the AP had given the world an extra 24 hours' peace.

The V-E Day episode typified the kind of conflict between government and journalism that would grow more common in the years to come—the era of the Cold War, Vietnam, Watergate.

For the AP, the postwar world was a wider world.

Washington, Nov. 29, 1989 – White House correspondent Terry Hunt (fourth from right) scribbles notes as President George Bush briefs members of the press on his agenda for an upcoming summit with Soviet President Mikhail S. Gorbachev.

The big European news agencies—"the cartel," Cooper called them—had long frozen the AP out of the international news marketplace. But Reuters, the biggest, finally conceded a freer hand to the American agency in the mid-1930s, and the war's end left the AP in a strong position to sell its news in dozens of countries. By 1950, the number of overseas customers had more than doubled.

Domestically, too, the cooperative was suddenly stronger.

Under old AP bylaws, members could—and did—veto applications for membership by other newspapers in their own cities. A 1945 Supreme

Court decision struck down this "exclusivity" rule on antitrust grounds.

Ironically, this ruling forcing a change in AP bylaws helped the organization, enabling it to recruit more fee-paying newspapers.

"It provided the bankroll that let the AP go to town," Kansas City publisher and board member Roy Roberts later observed.

It went to town, for example, by establishing the first all-sports wire. And the bankroll was fattening further because a wary board, after lengthy debate, had allowed the AP to start selling news to the upstart medium in town— radio—in 1942.

This expanding news empire had in Cooper an administrator with a highly personal, one-man leadership style. In 1948, the board opted for a new kind of AP chief, installing as general manager Frank Starzel, a cautious delegator who had risen through the ranks.

Beyond "50 Rock," a new kind of conflict—a Cold War—was engulfing the world. Its first crisis unfolded in Germany in 1948, as reported by the AP's George Bria:

BERLIN, SEPT. 18 (AP)—American and British Air Forces sent 895 cargo flights into Soviet-blockaded Berlin today in an awesome demonstration of peacetime air power.

The Berlin Blockade ended the following spring, but U.S.-Soviet hostility kept the Iron Curtain a focus of news and danger for foreign correspondents.

In Czechoslovakia in 1951, the AP's William N. Oatis, a mild-mannered but dogged journalist, was arrested by Communist authorities and charged with spying, for reporting news from Prague to the world.

Oatis was a particular threat, the prosecutor said, because of "his insistence on obtaining only accurate, correct, verified information." He spent two years in prison.

Halfway around the world, in Korea, the Cold War turned hot and the AP again deployed its own army. Many were veterans of World War II coverage, including Relman Morin and Don Whitehead, who jointly won a Pulitzer for their reporting from the remote new conflict.

Whitehead won a second Pulitzer for a story on President-elect Dwight D. Eisenhower's secret trips to Korea.

Back home, the peerless "Pat" Morin also collected a second Pulitzer for his gripping, first-hand reports from Little Rock, Ark., on the desegregation of schools.

It was one of the headline events of an era when America seemed never to hold still, ever to be remaking itself.

Still another new medium, television, was now in the nation's living rooms, and so was the AP, a news giant setting the agenda for everyone from the evening anchor to the small-town daily, helping Americans keep up with themselves through the civil rights movement and the "New Frontier" presidency, through women's liberation and youth revolution, through years of U.S. prosperity, prowess and problems.

In one sense, it all climaxed triumphantly on a July Sunday in 1969 with the AP flash, "Man on moon." But in another sense, this era of excitement ended in scandal, war and protest, in the stories labeled simply "Watergate" and "Vietnam."

HOUSTON, AUG. 15, 1992 – AP staff members edit photos at a computer under the main camera platform in the Astrodome, site of the 1992 Republican National Convention. A digital camera tethered to the electronic darkroom enabled editors under the platform to see the pictures instantly and transmit them to newspapers moments later. From left are: Mike Bauer, communications director; David Rocha, photo editor; Jim Gerberich, electronic technology coordinator; and Ron Edmonds, AP Washington photographer.

KHAN YUNIS, GAZA, NOV. 30, 1993 – AP photographer Jerome Delay, right, is shot and bruised in the leg with a rubber-covered steel bullet as he and AP photographer Adel al-Hana, center, are caught in a clash between Palestinians throwing stones and Israeli soldiers.

The conflict in Southeast Asia set American against American, government against the press, reporter against editor.

"Vietnam is neither black nor white, nor clear, nor simple," AP's Wes Gallagher noted. "When the correspondent reports the confusion, he satisfies neither the reader nor the government, but that's his job."

Gallagher, the World War II stalwart, had been elevated to AP general manager in 1962. He brought with him hands-on enthusiasm, a determination to fit the AP news operation to the times. He established a Washington investigative team, for example, and a "Mod Squad" to report on social trends.

But Vietnam, for one tumultuous decade, overshadowed all.

At AP headquarters, Gallagher and his editors fended off criticism of "negative" AP war reporting, from both the U.S. government and some member publishers. In the field, meanwhile, AP reporters had to contend with determined efforts by the U.S. military to control the news.

In Washington, the president who pledged to end the war soon was sinking in scandal, in a long-running drama whose complexities and cover-ups tested the resources and the mettle of the AP and the rest of the news media.

LIMA, PERU, APRIL 15, 1997 – APTV cameraman Mauricio Munoz aims his video camera at the Japanese ambassador's residence where Tupac Amaru rebels were holding more than 70 hostages. The four-month-long crisis ended when government commandos staged a raid on the residence, killing the captors. AP photographers, writers and video crews manned a rooftop lookout 24 hours a day during the siege.

White House correspondent Frank Cormier wrote the final act the night of Aug. 8, 1974:

WASHINGTON (AP)—President Nixon resigned Thursday night, telling the nation he acted to help heal the wounds of Watergate and to give America "a full-time president" in Gerald R. Ford.

SARAJEVO, BOSNIA-HERZEGOVINA, JUNE 11, 1997 – AP staff members hitch a ride aboard a U.S. Army Black Hawk helicopter to cover a training exercise of NATO peacekeeping forces in Bosnia. From left are photographer Rikard Larma, correspondent Aida Cerkez and APTV cameraman Eldar Emric.

As challenging as they were for news coverage, the Gallagher years were revolutionary for news technology.

In the early 1970s, the AP was the first news agency to install a large-scale computer system for writing, editing and transmitting its report. Teletype, the 60-word-a-minute tortoise, gave way to a "DataStream" hare that eventually ran 200 times faster.

In 1974, the once-wary relationship with broadcasters bore new fruit: an audio news service produced by the AP. Photo transmission went "digital" in the late 1970s, and in 1980 the AP pioneered satellite transmission of news.

For workaday reporters and photographers, the technological gem was the combination, by the late 1980s, of laptop computers, portable negative transmitters and satellite phones, enabling them to dial out from anywhere to file on-the-spot copy and pictures.

Thus equipped, the AP was ready for the disorderly "new world order" of the 1990s, a time of unpredictable explosions in unlikely corners of the globe—like Somalia.

When U.S. Marines came ashore there in 1992, in a city with no electricity, no telephones and little of anything else, the AP's Tina Susman could immediately relay word to the world:

MOGADISHU, Somalia (AP)—Mobbed by the media but meeting no resistance, American troops landed by moonlight and television lights early Wednesday and extended heavily armed helping hands to feed Somalia's starving millions.

But even the best technology doesn't eliminate the danger in dangerous assignments. Two years later, Susman was kidnapped, caught up in the clan violence wracking Mogadishu.

For 20 days, until she was freed, the kidnapping recalled for the AP the slow-motion agony of one of its greatest trials as an institution—the nearly seven-year-long captivity of Terry Anderson.

CARTAGENA DEL CHAIRA, COLOMBIA, JUNE 15, 1997 – AP Bogota correspondent Christopher Torchia, right, watches as a guerrilla of the nation's largest rebel group, left, escorts one of 70 captured soldiers to a ceremony at which the soldiers were released.

Anderson, chief AP Middle East correspondent, was abducted in Beirut one March morning in 1985 and bundled off to a dark hell as a hostage.

His Lebanese captors' demands were ever-changing; the AP's efforts to free him were nonstop, involving the U.S. and other governments, quiet intermediaries and public pleas.

The ordeal finally ended through U.N. mediation, in late 1991, and Anderson returned to a joyous homecoming at "50 Rock."

But the perils of reporting will never end. In the first half of the 1990s alone, six AP staff members lost their lives pursuing their calling, including correspondent Sharon Herbaugh in war-shattered Afghanistan, the first woman to die in service to the AP and news.

That list also included four photographers—

183

not surprising, perhaps, in a period when AP photojournalists, so often the "point men" in a violent world, also won six Pulitzer Prizes.

In 1906, an avid newspaper reader, addressing a banquet of AP member publishers, paid tribute to the power of their cooperative.

"There are only two forces that can carry light to all corners of the globe," Mark Twain said, "the sun in the heavens and The Associated Press down here. I may seem to be flattering the sun, but I do not mean it so; I am meaning only to be just and fair all around. You speak with a million voices; no one can reach so many races, so many hearts and intellects."

What might the former printer's apprentice have thought of the AP at century's end, in the Internet Age?

In the 1990s, the AP is a window on the world for hundreds of millions of people, reaching more than 15,000 news outlets in 112 nations. In the United States, it has more than 1,500 newspaper members and serves 6,000 radio and television stations.

This decade brought a changed competitive landscape, domestically and internationally, as technology opened doors to new players and the habits and boundaries of the old world fell away.

No one, however, matched the AP in what it had to offer.

Under Boccardi, a onetime New York newspaper editor who became president in 1985, the organization has grown in many directions.

In 1994 it introduced APTV, a global news video service based in London, and AP All News Radio, a 24-hour audio format that allows even the smallest radio station to carry nonstop news.

In photos, it remains the industry leader. Filmless digital cameras, developed with Kodak, coupled with state-of-the-art digital darkrooms, enable AP photojournalists to get pictures to papers in minutes—from shutter release to arrival in far-off newsrooms.

A graphics department closely tracks the news and supplies charts and other illustrations to hundreds of newspapers. A global business wire, operated with Dow Jones, serves subscribers in more than 40 countries. AP Information Services

ABOARD THE USS *CONSTITUTION*, JULY 21, 1997 – AP Boston photographer Elise Amendola transmits photos from the deck of the 19th-century warship the USS *Constitution*, sailing 10 miles off the coast of Massachusetts. Amendola shot with a filmless digital camera and used a cellular telephone to transmit the pictures from her laptop computer.

produces topical wires for specialist clients. And, in 1996, AP Multimedia Services led the cooperative into the newest medium of all, the Internet. On the Web sites of many newspapers, an AP text-picture-sound link, dubbed "The WIRE," is the gateway to continuously updated news of the nation and the world.

A broad, successful business development program, capitalizing on AP skills and capacities, developed major new sources of revenue to support the cooperative's activities. Enough niche businesses have been built—subleasing satellite time, forwarding newspaper ads, transmitting others' news on its network—to allow the AP to cross a threshold: The bulk of revenues no longer comes, as it once did, from the monthly "assessments" levied on domestic newspaper members for the basic service.

Those assessments were finally modernized in 1984 under Keith Fuller, Boccardi's predecessor as president, and then-Board Chairman Frank Batten, of Landmark Communications. Long set under an arcane, population-based formula, the assessment rates were changed to reflect a newspaper's circulation.

Even the smallest papers have a voice in running the AP.

Three directors on the 24-seat board come

from cities with populations of under 50,000. Broadcasters hold four board seats.

The members provide not just administrative oversight, but also much of the cooperative's domestic news underpinning.

The 143 AP bureaus across the United States receive an electronic stream of articles offered by newspapers and broadcasters, news of potential interest beyond their localities. The best are refined and updated by AP rewrite editors for state news wires, where they join reports from the AP's own state-level correspondents.

Then the best of these are sent to New York, to join the mix of news from AP correspondents in Washington and 93 international bureaus, in a flow of copy that New York editors cull, trim, retouch and send on its way to members and subscribers on six continents. With photos, with audio feeds, with video, the story the AP tells every minute of every day is nothing less than the never-ending story of what the world is up to.

The price of eggs. The president's news conference. African massacres and five-day forecasts. A debate in the state assembly. A near-disaster in space.

For breadth of coverage, journalism has nothing else like the AP report. But what about depth? In the rush of headlines, does the AP too seldom stop to dig?

Editors will long remember that during Vietnam the first report of the My Lai massacre was the AP's, but it was forgettably brief and not followed up. And on the century's biggest Washington scandal, Watergate, the AP, like most other news organizations, largely reported what a few others were uncovering.

Top AP editors and staff have worked to overcome the image of a bulletin service, to better explore the "why" in the news, along with delivering the "who, what, where and when."

"We want to make it impossible for anybody to disparage anything we do with the old insult that it's just 'wire service journalism,'" Boccardi told AP members at their annual meeting in 1995.

And a sampling from the 1990s shows that the river of copy does, indeed, run deep as well as wide:

The AP reported, minute by minute, the inner-

LITTLE ROCK, ARK., SEPT. 25, 1997 – AP staff photographer Eric Draper uses a laptop computer to transmit his photos outside Little Rock Central High School during ceremonies marking the 40th anniversary of the school's intergration.

city rioting in Los Angeles. But it also produced, over two years, a series of thoughtful articles, "Separate Nations," on race relations in America.

Its photographers captured historic moments on the White House lawn. But its Washington staff, armed with computer analyses, also painstakingly detailed failures in federal workplace inspections.

It instantaneously informed the world that the Marines had landed in Mogadishu. But it also pieced together a powerful photo essay, evolving over weeks, on a single Somali refugee's quest for a new life.

The world's biggest source of news, vital institution that it is, will always come under criticism, and profit from it.

But as turn-of-the-century New York publisher Oswald Garrison Villard once noted, "I have yet to learn of a constructive suggestion as to something better to take the place of The Associated Press."

The world has changed, and the news with it. The urgent hum of dots and dashes summoning editors to telegraph desks is now the calm click of a computer mouse.

But the job, after 150 years, is the same. And the words—of anticipation, expectation, trust— will probably never change.

"Check the wire. What does the AP say?"

Greg English

DAMASCUS, SYRIA, DEC. 4, 1991 – Terry Anderson, AP's chief Middle East correspondent and the longest-held American hostage in Lebanon, raises his arms at a news conference at the Syrian Foreign Ministry the day of his release. Anderson had been a captive for six and a half years.

ACKNOWLEDGMENTS / CREDITS

This book celebrating 150 years of AP history and photographs has been guided from the outset by a team from The Associated Press and Harry N. Abrams, Inc. These included AP's Vincent Alabiso, vice president and executive photo editor; Victoria Smith, director of Corporate Communications; Kelly Smith Tunney, assistant to the president; Chuck Zoeller, director of the AP Photo Library; Eric Himmel, senior editor and director of new media for Harry N. Abrams, Inc.; and Raymond P. Hooper, art director, special projects for Abrams.

ON THE PHOTOGRAPHS
AND THE PHOTOGRAPHERS

The photographs were selected from the files of The Associated Press NewsPhoto Library, one of the world's largest collections of news and documentary photography, holding millions of images.

Every effort has been made to establish and confirm photographers' names, particularly on older photos. Photo credits by name were not routinely recorded in the early decades. Many AP photos were filed with just the photographer's initials—or no credit at all. Photo credits have since become the norm. Contemporary AP photos are virtually always transmitted with full credits, and many publications have now adopted the practice of crediting in print both The Associated Press and the photographer by name.

PHOTO ACKNOWLEDGMENTS

Selecting, editing and printing the photos for this book required the cooperation and assistance of dozens of people both inside and outside the AP.

The staff of AP's NewsPhoto Library carried out the enormous task of photo research. Photo librarian Stephen Ciaschi started, and continues, groundbreaking research into some of the AP's earliest original photographs. His work greatly contributed to the development of this book. Librarians Ronnie Farley, Carolyn Lessard, Jim Supanick and Jocko Weyland also conducted essential research, as did library staffers Joseph M. Kuntz and Stanley Rubinstein. All library staffers contributed in their daily work as researchers and archivists: Maggie Bergara, Dewitt Bouker, Sue Boyle, Yolanda Cancell, Dick Carroll, Kenny Cifone, Anne Gillen, Claudia Hird, Todd Hodgman, Margie Jacobs, Clairisse Jud, Nancy Jung, Maura Lynch, Walter Mosby, Paul Rose, Sean Silleck and Julia Wilson.

Additional research was provided by AP's London Photo Library, particularly Joan Fisher, Jane Gowman and Michael Hollingshead.

A team of AP editors shaped the selection of photos. Santos Chaparro, Bob Daugherty, Brian Horton, Mike Martinez, Sally Stapleton, Tom Stathis and Bernadette Tuazon all played key roles. In AP's London bureau both Horst Faas and Mike Feldman made important contributions, as did Denis Paquin in Tokyo.

Hal Buell, former executive NewsPhotos editor, now retired, offered the perspective of his years of experience and became a source of historical information that might otherwise have been lost forever. Administrative Assistant Vivian Bonatti provided valuable assistance in locating photographers.

Staff retoucher Gulnara Samoilova performed meticulous digital and hand reconstruction of prints and negatives. Additional print retouching was carried out by David Joseph of Joseph & Dzurella.

The photo printing staff was coordinated by darkroom supervisor Tim Donnelly.

Staff color printers were Jesus Medina, Guy Palmiotto, Mauricio Penneherra and Constantine "Gus" Polichron.

Archival black-and-white printer was Brian Young of Phototechnica. Additional darkroom work was completed by Time-Life Photo Laboratories, Raffi Custom Photo Lab, and Metro Imaging, London. Archival negative duplication was carried out by Michael Hager of Museum Photographics, Rochester, N.Y.

Also providing lab service and support were AP staffers

Nick Andriani, John Carucci, Angie Coqueran, Anders Goldfarb, Don Hattley, Seong-Chang Hong, Doug Jeffries, Brian Killigrew, Wilfred Kolin, Joe Lonergan, James Ryan, Wilfred Salomon, Patricia Wall, Curtis Yantz and Irwan Yulianto.

Photo researcher Harris Lewine advised throughout this project. Additional research was conducted by Melissa LeBoeuf of Eddie Adams Inc., Nancy Weinstock of *The New York Times*, W.C. Burdick of the Baseball Hall of Fame and Allan Goodrich of the John F. Kennedy Library. Photo researcher Gail Buckland also contributed her expertise, and AP New York staff photographer Mark Lennihan provided studio photography.

Our most sincere thanks go to the worldwide family of AP photographers past and present, too few of whom could be included in this collection. Without their passionate commitment and dedication to the ideals of photojournalism, this book would not have been possible.

EDITORIAL ACKNOWLEDGMENTS

Writing and research were efforts shared enthusiastically by all levels of the AP staff, domestically and internationally. Bureau chiefs, staff members and retirees from around the world volunteered time in helping AP collect and sort anecdotes and memorabilia, only a small portion of which could be included in this volume. Special Correspondent Jules Loh, now retired, spearheaded initial book research with the help of Norman Goldstein, director of AP Newsfeatures special projects, Special Correspondent Hugh A. Mulligan, Broadcast Deputy Director and Managing Editor Brad Kalbfeld and National Writer Ted Anthony.

Ann Bertini, administrative assistant in the AP President's Office, was coordinator for captions and research and worked closely with Rachel Tsutsumi at Abrams. They were assisted by Arnold Wilkinson, information specialist, and Susan James, head information specialist, in AP's News and Information Research Center, Susan Hoffmann in Enterprise, and Eva Tatarczyk and Rita Sullivan of the AP President's Office. Janis Magin, special projects manager for AP Corporate Communications, and Lilo Jedelhauser, director of Corporate Events, helped research historic AP staff and company files.

PULITZERS

The Pulitzer Prizes, American journalism's most prestigious honor, were established by Joseph Pulitzer in 1917 and are presented annually for outstanding achievement in news coverage.

The Associated Press has won 43 Pulitzer Prizes, more than any other news organization in categories for which it can compete. These include 18 Pulitzer Prizes for writing and 25 for pictures. Sixty-one men and women are included in those prizes, 19 writers and 42 photographers.

1922 - KIRKE L. SIMPSON, for a series of stories on the burial of the Unknown Soldier at Arlington National Cemetery in Virginia.

1933 - FRANCIS (FRANK) A. JAMIESON, for a news beat on finding the body of the kidnapped baby of aviator Charles Lindbergh and for stories on the search for the killer.

1937 - HOWARD W. BLAKESLEE, for reporting on the Harvard tricentennial celebration.

1939 - LOUIS P. LOCHNER, for news reports from Nazi Germany.

1942 - LAURENCE E. ALLEN, for World War II reporting, especially stories on the bombing of the British aircraft carrier *Illustrious.*

1943 - FRANK NOEL, for a picture of a survivor of a torpedo attack begging for water from a lifeboat in World War II.

1944 - DANIEL DELUCE, for a series of stories from Yugoslavia disclosing the strength of the Tito movement.

1944 - FRANK FILAN, for a picture of a blasted Japanese pillbox on Tarawa during World War II.

1945 - HAL BOYLE, for columns and stories from the North African and European theaters during World War II.

1945 - JOE ROSENTHAL, for a picture of U.S. Marines raising the American flag on Iwo Jima during World War II.

1947 - EDDY GILMORE, for news reports from Russia, especially an interview with Soviet leader Joseph Stalin.

1947 - ARNOLD HARDY, for his photo of a girl leaping to her death in a hotel fire.

1951 - MAX DESFOR, for a picture of Korean War refugees in flight over ruins of the Taedong River bridge.

1951 - RELMAN MORIN AND DON WHITEHEAD, for reports from the Korean War.

1952 - JOHN HIGHTOWER, for reporting of international affairs.

1953 - DON WHITEHEAD, for a story on President-elect Dwight D. Eisenhower's secret trips to Korea.

1954 - VIRGINIA SCHAU, for a photo of the rescue of two men trapped in a truck after it plunged off a bridge in California.

1958 - RELMAN MORIN, for reports on school desegregation rioting at Little Rock, Ark.

1961 - LYNN HEINZERLING, for reports on the early stages of the Congo crisis and analysis of other African events.

1962 - PAUL VATHIS, for a picture of President John F. Kennedy and former President Dwight D. Eisenhower walking at Camp David following the failed 1961 invasion of Cuba.

1964 - MALCOLM BROWNE, for reports from the Vietnam War.

1965 - HORST FAAS, for photos from the Vietnam War.

1966 - PETER ARNETT, for reports from the Vietnam War.

1967 - JACK THORNELL, for a picture of civil rights activist James Meredith after he was shot near Hernando, Miss.

1969 - EDWARD (EDDIE) ADAMS, for a picture of Vietnamese Brig. Gen. Nguyen Ngoc Loan executing a Viet Cong prisoner on a Saigon street.

1970 - STEVE STARR, for a picture of armed black students emerging after their 36-hour occupation of a Cornell University building.

1972 - HORST FAAS AND MICHEL LAURENT, for a series of pictures of tortures and executions in Bangladesh.

1973 - HUYNH CONG (NICK) UT, for a picture of a Vietnamese girl fleeing in terror after a napalm attack.

1974 - ANTHONY K. ROBERTS, for a picture sequence made during an alleged kidnapping attempt in Hollywood.

1974 - SLAVA (SAL) VEDER, for a picture of a U.S. Air Force officer being greeted by his family after being held as a prisoner of war in Vietnam.

1977 - WALTER R. MEARS, for reports on the 1976 presidential campaign and election.

1977 - NEAL ULEVICH, for a series of pictures showing bloody fighting between police and students in Bangkok, Thailand.

1978 - J. ROSS BAUGHMAN, for a series of pictures showing white Rhodesian soldiers beating and torturing black nationalist guerrillas.

1982 - RON EDMONDS, for a series of pictures showing the attempted assassination of U.S. President Ronald Reagan.

1982 - SAUL PETT, for a series of stories on the bureaucracy of the federal government.

1983 - BILL FOLEY, for a series of pictures of victims and survivors of the massacre of Palestinians in a refugee camp in Beirut.

1991 - GREG MARINOVICH, for a series of pictures showing the brutal killing of a man believed to be a Zulu Inkatha supporter in South Africa.

1992 - OLGA SHALYGIN, LIU HEUNG SHING, CZAREK SOKOLOWSKI, BORIS YURCHENKO AND ALEXANDER ZEMLI-ANICHENKO, for a series of pictures on the attempted coup in the Soviet Union and the collapse of the Communist regime.

1993 - SCOTT APPLEWHITE, RICHARD DREW, GREG GIBSON, DAVID LONG-STREATH, DOUG MILLS, MARCY NIGHS-WANDER, AMY SANCETTA, STEPHAN SAVOIA, REED SAXON AND LYNNE SLADKY, for a series of pictures from the 1992 U.S. presidential campaign.

1995 - JAVIER BAULUZ, JEAN-MARC BOUJU, JACQUELINE ARZT LARMA AND KARSTEN THIELKER, for photos of the ethnic violence in Rwanda.

1995 - MARK FRITZ, for reports on the ethnic violence in Rwanda.

1996 - CHARLES PORTER IV, for his photo of a firefighter cradling an infant victim of the Oklahoma City bombing.

1997 - ALEXANDER ZEMLIANICHENKO, for his photo of Russian President Boris Yeltsin dancing at a rock concert in Rostov during the Russian presidential campaign.

HONOR ROLL

These 23 journalists lost their lives covering stories for the AP:

1876 - MARK KELLOGG, a reporter for the *Bismarck Tribune* and AP, died at the Battle of Little Bighorn.

1898 - NEWSMAN AMBROSE W. LYMAN contracted yellow fever while covering the Spanish-American War in Cuba and died on returning to the United States.

1904 - NEWSMAN HENRY J. MIDDLETON died of dysentery in China while covering the Russo-Japanese War.

1938 - NEWSMAN EDWARD J. NEIL died in Saragossa, Spain, two days after being fatally wounded by a shell that exploded in front of the parked car he was seated in during the Spanish Civil War.

1942 - NEWSMAN DANIEL WITT HANCOCK, the first AP reporter to die during World War II, was killed when Japanese bombers attacked and sank the Dutch refugee ship he was aboard in the Indian Ocean.

1943 - NEWSMAN EDWARD H. (HARRY) CROCKETT was killed during World War II when the British ship he was on was torpedoed by enemy warships in the Mediterranean Sea.

1944 - NEWSMAN ASAHEL (ACE) BUSH was the first correspondent to lose his life in the Philippines during World War II. He died when a Japanese bomb struck the American-occupied capital of Tacloban, on the Philippine island of Leyte.

1944 - NEWSMAN GEORGE BEDE IRVIN was killed after photographing an aerial bombardment north of St. Lo, France, during a barrage that signaled the start of the Allied drive out of Normandy during World War II.

1945 - NEWSMAN JOSEPH MORTON was captured and executed by the Nazis at the Mauthausen concentration camp near Linz, Austria, during World War II. Morton had accompanied a group of American intelligence officers on a mission in Slovakia during the fall of 1944 to investigate a revolt that liberated downed Allied airmen from enemy prison camps.

1950 - NEWSMAN WILLIAM R. MOORE was killed by mortar fire in Korea while trying to care for an Army lieutenant wounded in a Communist attack near Chinju during the Korean War.

1958 - NEWSMAN DANIEL J. COUGHLIN died in the crash of an Air Force jet attempting to break speed records at Westover (Mass.) Air Force Base.

1965 - PHOTOGRAPHER BERNARD KOLENBERG died in the collision of two fighter-bombers during the Vietnam War.

1965 - PHOTOGRAPHER HUYNH THANH MY was killed while covering a battle in the Mekong Delta in South Vietnam during the Vietnam War.

1968 - PHOTOGRAPHER KLAUS FRINGS died two days after being struck in the head by a rock during a clash between police and students at a demonstration outside the Munich offices of the newspaper *Bild-Zeitung*.

1969 - PHOTOGRAPHER OLIVER NOONAN was killed when the evacuation helicopter he boarded to carry wounded American soldiers was shot down over the jungle about 30 miles south of Da Nang, Vietnam.

1971 - PHOTOGRAPHER HENRI HUET was killed when his helicopter was shot down over Laos in Southeast Asia.

1971 - PHOTOGRAPHER DENNIS LEE ROYLE died in a helicopter crash over the English Channel while covering naval exercises conducted by the North Atlantic Treaty Organization.

1993 - SHARON HERBAUGH, the first AP newswoman and bureau chief to die on assignment, was killed in a helicopter crash in the central Afghanistan mountains, 100 miles north of Kabul. Herbaugh had spent three years covering the Afghan civil war and its aftermath.

1993 - PHOTOGRAPHER HANSJOERG (HANSI) KRAUSS was killed by a Somali mob while covering the civil war near Mogadishu, Somalia.

1993 - ALI IBRAHIM MURSAL, an AP driver and translator, was killed defending another AP staffer from a thief in Somalia.

1993 - PHOTOGRAPHER ANDREI SOLOVIEV was shot to death during a battle between Abkhazian and Georgian forces for control of Sukhumi in the breakaway region of Abkhazia.

1994 - PHOTOGRAPHER ABDUL SHARIFF was shot to death while covering a congregation of African National Congress leaders visiting Katlehong, South Africa.

1995 - FARKHAD KERIMOV, an APTV videographer, was shot and killed covering the war in Chechnya.

CHAIRMEN / PRESIDENTS

Founders of The Associated Press, 1848

James Gordon Bennett, Frederick Hudson
New York Herald

James Watson Webb, Henry J. Raymond
New York Courier and Enquirer

Gerard Hallock, David Hale
New York Journal of Commerce

Horace Greeley
New York Tribune

Moses Beach
New York Sun

Eustace Brooks, James Brooks
New York Express

Since the AP's incorporation in the state of
New York in 1900, these news executives
have led the cooperative.

Chairmen of the Board

1900–38	Frank B. Noyes The (Washington, D.C.) Evening Star
1938–57	Robert McLean The (Philadelphia) Evening Bulletin
1957–63	Benjamin M. McKelway The (Washington, D.C.) Evening Star
1963–77	Paul Miller Times-Union (Rochester, N.Y.)
1977–82	Jack Tarver The Atlanta Journal-Constitution
1982–87	Frank Batten The (Norfolk, Va.) Ledger-Star
1987–92	William J. Keating The Cincinnati (Ohio) Enquirer
1992–97	Frank A. Daniels Jr. The (Raleigh, N.C.) News & Observer
1997–	Donald E. Newhouse The (Newark, N.J.) Star-Ledger

Presidents (The title was General Manager until 1972.)

1900–21	Melville E. Stone General Manager
1921–25	Frederick Roy Martin General Manager
1925–48	Kent Cooper General Manager
1948–62	Frank J. Starzel General Manager
1962–76	Wes Gallagher President and General Manager
1976–85	Keith Fuller President and General Manager
1985–	Louis D. Boccardi President and CEO

BOARD OF DIRECTORS

The Associated Press
Board of Directors 1997–98

Donald E. Newhouse, Chairman
President, Advance Publications Inc.
The (Newark, N.J.) Star-Ledger

William R. Burleigh, Vice Chairman
President & CEO
The E.W. Scripps Company

Roy E. (Gene) Bell
President & CEO
The San Diego Union-Tribune

Judith W. Brown
Editor
The (New Britain, Conn.) Herald

John J. Curley
Chairman & CEO
Gannett Co. Inc.

Reginald Davenport
Executive Vice President
New York Times Co. Regional
Newspaper Group

R. Victor Dix
Chairman, Dix Communications
The (Wooster, Ohio) Daily Record

David E. Easterly
President & COO
Cox Enterprises Inc.

Larry Franklin
President & CEO
Harte-Hanks Communications Inc.

Stephen Hamblett
Chairman, CEO & Publisher
The Providence (R.I.) Journal Co.

Richard J. Harrington
Chief Operating Officer
The Thomson Corp.

Gregg K. Jones
Co-publisher
The Greeneville (Tenn.) Sun

Andrew Lack
President
NBC News

John W. Madigan
Chairman, President & CEO
Tribune Company

John G. Montgomery
President & CEO, Montgomery
Communications Inc.
The (Junction City, Kan.)
Daily Union

Burl Osborne
President, Publishing Div.,
A.H. Belo Corp.
Publisher & CEO
The Dallas Morning News

Orage Quarles III
Publisher
The Modesto (Calif.) Bee

P. Anthony Ridder
Chairman & CEO
Knight-Ridder Inc.

G. William Ryan
President & CEO
Post-Newsweek Stations Inc.

Mary Schurz
Editor & Publisher
The (Danville, Ky.)
Advocate-Messenger

Lissa Walls Vahldiek
Chief Operating Officer
Southern Newspapers Inc.

George W. Wilson
President
Concord (N.H.) Monitor

VICE PRESIDENTS

Associated Press Vice Presidents

Patrick T. O'Brien
Senior Vice President, Business and Finance
and CFO

William E. Ahearn
Vice President and Executive Editor

Vincent Alabiso
Vice President and Executive Photo Editor

James M. Donna
Vice President and Director of
Human Resources

Claude E. Erbsen
Vice President and Director of World Services

John Reid
Vice President and Director of
Communications and Technology

Wick Temple
Vice President and Director of Newspaper
Membership

James R. Williams
Vice President and Director of Broadcast
Services

Walter R. Mears
Vice President and Special Correspondent

INDEX